WOMEN IN GERMAN YEARBOOK 1

Feminist Studies and
German Culture

Edited by
Marianne Burkhard
Edith Waldstein

UNIVERSITY
PRESS OF
AMERICA

LANHAM • NEW YORK • LONDON

TABLE OF CONTENTS

PREFACE

With the present publication, the first volume of a continuing Yearbook, the Coalition of Women in German is once again broadening the scope of its activities. Having organized not only an annual conference since 1976, but also sessions at the AATG and MLA Conventions since 1977, WiG has regularly contributed to the professional enterprise of these conferences, i.e. the direct exchange of scholarly ideas on a national and international level. As important and productive as such conference discussions are, they have limits which are felt more clearly in a time when means for attending conferences are diminishing, while research in the area of Women's Studies in Germanistik is rapidly expanding. This research has opened new areas of inquiry and developed new methodologies, so as to gain better insight into long neglected areas of our literary and cultural heritage as well as our pedagogical activities. The Women in German Yearbook is a response to the growing interest in Women's Studies in German literature and culture, which has resulted in the need to disseminate relevant materials, studies, hypotheses and results.

The present volume is representative of the varied areas in which our members are working. Certainly literary studies are a central concern, but at the same time we also feel the need to discuss notions about and attitudes toward women in contemporary society, so as to continue the all important reflective process and dialogue, which will, we hope, lead to a more accurate understanding of women's existence in all spheres of life. It is for this reason that we have included essays not only on literary works and the teaching of grammar and culture, but also on the problems experienced

v

by female guestworkers in the Federal Republic of Germany and on the dynamics of gender in the publications of the West German Peace Movement. By way of introduction, we have also included an article on the history and aims of our organization.

Marianne Burkhard
University of Illinois
at Urbana-Champaign

Edith Waldstein
Massachusetts Institute
of Technology

Jeanette Clausen

The Coalition of Women in German:
An Interpretive History and Celebration*

In this essay I review the history of the Coalition of Women in German: our beginnings as an organization; goals and projects; relationships to the Women's Studies movement and the women's movement in
general; relationships to other academic associations;
the structure of the organization; our accomplishments
and our goals for the future. This is a subjective
report; my colleagues in WiG would see certain things
differently or with a different emphasis, since our
experiences are not identical. The history of WiG con-
sists of the concrete experiences and struggles we
have shared and continue to share. I write in solidarity with and in celebration of WiG and our work toward
a feminist transformation of our lives and our profession.

Early Days

WiG's beginnings are embedded in developments in
the women's movement, both in the US and in Germany,
and in the growth of Women's Studies as an academic
area in the 1970s. Feminist Germanists meeting informally at the MLA and AATG conventions discovered shared
concerns and discussed their need for more communication with others interested in both Women's Studies
and German Studies. A discussion at the November 1974
MLA meeting led to the first organizational step: several women at the University of Wisconsin (Madison)
agreed to send out a newsletter announcing a special
meeting at the MLA convention that year. At that meeting, ideas for collective projects and plans for future conference programs were discussed. The topics
chosen reflect some of the major directions of Women's
Studies at the time: feminist critiques of teaching
materials, especially German textbooks; feminist pedagogy; feminist critiques of works by major authors,
and so on.

The name "Women in German" also came out of the
discussion at this first meeting. Women in German
was chosen over Germanistik, since the latter term
applies only to German Studies at postsecondary institutions and thus would seem to exclude high school

1

teachers and others not employed or studying at a university. Like the National Women's Studies Association (NWSA), founded in 1976-77, which aims to promote feminist education and research "at all educational levels and in every educational setting,"[1] the intent was to be more inclusive and democratic, to expand the traditional boundaries of the "academy". And, for much the same reasons that feminist academic programs were named Women's Studies, our organization is called Women in German, not "feminists," though the group's aim was explicitly feminist from the start. People believed, and not without reason, that the term "feminist" might scare away potential members, especially pre-feminist women ("I'm not a feminist but I believe in equal pay for equal work.") The name, and the abbreviation WiG, have since become firmly established.[2]

WiG Newsletter and Collective

The Women in German newsletter, which appeared regularly after that first (1974) issue, was important as a means of spreading information about the activities of the budding organization. A collective of students and one professor (later two) at the University of Wisconsin assumed responsibility for preparing and distributing the newsletter. After the first three issues, it became clear that the newsletter could no longer be sent free of charge, and subscribers were asked to pay a minimal fee. The list of subscribers grew quickly, to over two hundred in two years. Current (1983) paid membership is about 350.

Besides reports on meetings, conference announcements, calls for papers, announcements of new publications, etc., the newsletter also contained information about the women's movement in Germany. It was through the WiG newsletter that many of us first heard of the West German feminist magazines Courage and Emma, about the Women's Summer Universities in Berlin (Frauensommerunis, since 1976), about German feminist song groups, women's bookstores, cafes, and many other cultural and political projects and events not reported in other feminist publications (let alone the academic journals of our discipline) in the US. At the time (mid-1970s), Women's Studies programs in the US, which often originated through the efforts of students and faculty in disciplines such as English, Communications, History, Psychology

2

and Sociology, were more ethnocentric than today,
devoting relatively little attention to women's movements in other countries, or to national literatures
other than British and American. Thus, feminists in
the field of German Studies were doubly disadvantaged,
since our "first" discipline did not recognize Women's
Studies as a valid area of academic inquiry, and
Women's Studies had not yet developed an international
awareness.

For these reasons, the work of the Madison collective -- gathering material and writing reports for
the newsletter, maintaining mailing lists, planning
outreach efforts, keeping financial records -- was
vital to the new organization's growth and stability.
The collective was also tone-setting in certain respects. The newsletter remained in Madison until
1981.[3] Like so many feminist projects and organizations, the Coalition of Women in German was built
through women's unpaid work, a circumstance that
probably won't change in the forseeable future.

The WiG Conferences -- How it all Began

As already mentioned, the first Women in German
group meetings were held at MLA and AATG conventions,
but already in the first newsletter (1974) the possibility of a separate conference "für und unter uns"
had been mentioned. Feminist Germanists felt a need
for a space where we could pursue in depth the questions that most interested us, without the limita-
tions -- of time, form, content and public -- of
the existing associations' meetings. The fourth
issue of the newsletter contained a call for volun-
teers to organize such a conference; several women at
Miami University (Oxford, Ohio) took the initiative
to do so. The first WiG conference took place on a
weekend in September 1976 in Oxford. It was called
"Feminism and German Studies: An Interdisciplinary
Perspective," and was designated a "Retreat and
Symposium," announced in the newsletter as follows:
"Coming forward to retreat. Until now,
Women in German [gemeint ist das News-
letter] has been a thread connecting
us in scattered places. Now we will
come together, face to face, to strength-
en these connections and to make
sure that we don't retreat into academic isolation."
(WiG Newsletter No. 8, Sept. 1976,p.1)

I will discuss the annual conferences in some detail, since they are so basic to the organization's identity, projects and initiatives. I will begin with the format of the conferences, though it can't be totally separated from the content.

Formal and Organizational Aspects of the Conferences

The first WiG conference had been planned as a retreat so that the participants (about 30) could be together for the entire weekend (Friday evening through Sunday noon) to engage in open, unstructured discussion before and after the symposium. The symposium, which lasted one day, consisted of (more or less) traditional papers on a variety of topics; following each presentation, respondents addressed the issues from a feminist perspective. This format was important precisely because it was the first such conference, and not all those attending, including some of the presenters, were familiar with the assumptions and methods of feminist research.

On rereading the newsletter summaries of this conference, it seems clear that for many participants, the open discussions before and after the symposium, focusing on two broad topics (feminist pedagogy and feminist literary criticism), were more important than the formal papers. I quote from Sara Lennox' report on the feminist pedagogy discussion:
"What was most exciting...was the feeling
of support and solidarity which derived
from discovering that a great many women
were struggling to create an alternative
classroom situation which would reflect our
feminist principles. It was exciting as well
to discover that many of us felt that feminists should not only examine a different
subject matter, but that they should do
it in a different way... One discussion
participant indicated that she had attended many Women's Studies meetings,but had
never participated in a workshop which devoted so much attention to 'process' (i.e.,
the way in which a group activity takes
place in contrast to the subject with which
it is dealing), and she hoped that this
indicated a new direction for Women's
Studies as a whole."
(WiG Newsletter No. 9, Dec. 1976, p. 6).

4

At the time, the feelings of mutual involvement and the process-oriented atmosphere/discussion may have developed more or less spontaneously simply because it was the first opportunity for most participants to share their experiences with a group of like-minded women. In subsequent years there has been a more conscious effort to integrate attention to "process" into the conference. For example, the opening sessions have been devoted to open discussions of topics relating to the personal/political/professional, with such titles as "Personal and Professional Survival as a Woman Germanist" (1978), "Transforming the Structures of Our Lives and Our Work" (1980), "Sprache, Gefühl und Feminismus" (1981). The intent is to provide an opportunity for discussion of personal, individual concerns in a supportive atmosphere and, as much as possible, to give everyone (especially those attending for the first time) a chance to introduce herself and make contact with others. Clearly, group work will be affected if some participants feel like outsiders.

For similar reasons, it was decided after the second conference (1977) to abandon the traditional symposium format in favor of "Arbeitsgruppen," to "encourage greater involvement on the part of all participants and to eliminate the typical split between 'active' papergivers and a 'passive' audience" (WiG Newsletter No. 13, Nov. 1977, p. 1). The goal of collective work remains as a guiding principle but has been difficult to achieve, surely in large part because attendance at the conferences continues to increase (about 70 participants in 1982), changing the composition of the group each year, and making it more difficult for all those attending to contribute to discussions.

Thematic Foci, "Uncomfortable Topics"

A process-oriented atmosphere and efforts to bridge the active/passive split can be decisive for work on topics where consciousness-raising activities are necessary to stimulate new research or -- much as I dislike the expression -- to "legitimize" them. An illustration is the 1979 conference, where for the first time (somewhat belatedly) a session was devoted to the topic "Lesbian Themes in German Literature." The call for papers on this topic elicited only three presentations, all on Ingeborg Bachmann's story "Ein Schritt nach Gomorrha." Evelyn Beck, one of the session organizers, summarized the situation as follows:

5

I introduced the topic by emphasizing
that it makes no sense to study lesbian
images in texts without understanding what
it means/has meant to be a lesbian in our
society. Possibly the most significant
factor about the panel was that it took
place at all, that some of us at the meeting broke the taboos and spoke out as lesbians, expressing our solidarity with the
nation-wide march on Washington in support
of gay rights that took place that same
weekend [as the 1979 conference]. It is important to note that we did not select the
Bachmann story; it chose us. The fact that
three papers all focused on this one story
says a good deal about the dearth of
lesbian themes in the German literature in
print and about attitudes towards lesbianism
in Germany."
(WiG Newletter No. 20, Nov. 1979, pp.6-7).

The discussion focused not only on the "actual"
topic -- lesbians in German literature -- but also
on the discussion participants and our experiences,
biases, etc., all of these being part of why the topic
had previously not been raised, or only peripherally.
The group discussions were uncomfortable for some,
and weren't welcomed by everyone, but they presented
at least the potential for changes in attitudes and
awareness, which would not have been the case in a
discussion focusing only on texts. Similar situations
arose during sessions on "German-Jewish Women Writers"
(1981) and "Speaking the Unspeakable" (1982). The
latter illustrates an interesting tension surrounding
uncomfortable topics, a kind of approach/avoidance
reaction. I heard from many women who expressed interest in the "Speaking the Unspeakable" topic, yet
only five sent proposals in response to our call for
papers, and only two of those actually addressed the
topic. I believe these examples show how important
the conference sessions on "unspeakable" topics are:
it is clear that many women are interested and want
to be informed,but either don't have the confidence
to tackle the topics on their own, or simply have no
idea where to begin. Thus, these sessions help open
new areas of research, besides providing opportunities for us to deal with differences that might otherwise divide us.
    Other general considerations that have influenc-
ed the choice of conference session topics are:

1) striking a balance between theoretical and practical work, and between pedagogy and literature/cul-
ture; 2) covering the various literary periods in
German literature; 3) including perspectives from
other disciplines; 4) aiming for transformation of
traditional scholarship. Because of the "Arbeits-
gruppe" format, it is considered important to have
hands-on material -- bibliographies, abstracts, course
outlines, etc. -- available for all participants.

The goal of transformation has led to discussions of aesthetics almost every year: "Women and the
Aesthetic of the Positive Hero in GDR Literature"
(1977), "The Woman Question and Aesthetics" (1978),
"Women and Aesthetics" (1979), "The Forms of Our
Bodies" (How do women "write themselves" into the text)
(1980), "New Ways of Reading" (1981). As these examples suggest, the session topics for any given
year grow out of discussions at the previous year's
conference and continue them. The topics are decided
in a plenary session during the conference; these
sessions have become larger and longer each year and,
again, require much attention to process in order
to arrive at a consensus. Tensions can arise, for example, (but not only) because newcomers and "old-tim-
ers" may have different expectations, and we are always pressed for time, which makes reaching a consensus more difficult. The crucial factor is, in
my opinion, that our goal is a consensus, even
though we may sometimes have to settle for a compromise.

Working with Authors

We have invited a woman author to our conference
every year since 1980; of course, her work also influences the choice of topics to some extent. So far,
our guests have been Margot Schroeder (1980), Angelika
Mechtel (1981), Luise Rinser (1982), Barbara
Frischmuth (1983); Irmtraud Morgner and Helga Schütz
have accepted our invitation for 1984. These trips
have been financed with the help of the respective
cultural institutes (Goethe House, Austrian Institute, GDR Embassy). Other readings,mostly at universities, are also arranged for the authors to make the
trip more attractive to them and the institute.

Since the authors are with us during the entire
conference (which has expanded from a weekend to

7

three days, Thursday evening to Sunday noon),including meals and breaks as well as scheduled discussions, we get much more from their visits (and so do they) than from the customary "Dichterlesung." All our guests so far have participated energetically in discussions; they have helped us arrive at new approaches to reading and teaching their works and have been candid in responding to our interpretations of their writing, even at times coming to see their own work somewhat differently. There is mutual influence and benefit, which couldn't as easily take place under other conditions.

The authors' presence at the conferences is also related to intense discussions about language since 1980. Previously, everyone simply spoke either German or English according to her preference. In consideration of the German-speaking authors, however, there was a move to conduct more of the discussions in German (though presenters were still to have the choice of using the language they felt most comfortable with). This led to some problems we could not have forseen. We found that some women experienced speaking the one or the other language as alienating, especially in discussing issues that touched them personally. For example, in discussions of anti-semitism, some women whose native language is German found it problematic to speak German. Others (myself, for example) lack the appropriate German vocabulary for discussing feminism because we developed our feminist thinking in the US, or simply feel embarassed about the possibility of making mistakes. Still others argue that we should use German as the language of the conference "weil wir alle Germanistinnen sind." None of the concerns is trivial, most particularly since our goal of working collectively and respecting differences is taken seriously. What seems clear is that choosing one language over the other is both a personal and political decision which has to do with the individual woman's relationship to her native language and its history. The 1982 discussions of language led to a decision to organize the 1983 conference around the theme "Stimme suchen, Stimme finden."

Working with/against other Associations

We consider it important to make our feminist work visible in the larger associations, especially the MLA and the AATG. By arranging programs for the annual meetings of these organizations, we not only reach a wider audience; we also create opportunities for our members to present their work in a more supportive atmosphere. The women who arrange the sessions (ideally, an inexperienced person works with one who has done it before) acquire new skills and expertise. The issue of "legitimacy" also plays a role: what is presented "only" at the annual WiG conferences may more easily be discounted (by department chairs and deans) than a presentation at AATG or MLA. Our work in and with these associations is also "against" them, to the extent that the presence of our programs may lead to change.

Since 1977 WiG has had "allied organization" status in the MLA, which gives us a certain identity within the Association, and also more freedom: we can plan more effectively knowing we are assured of having a slot on the convention program each year, and our presence there has a certain permanence. Besides two programs at the annual MLA conventions, we have generally arranged two sessions for the AATG meetings also, except for years in which the AATG met in states that have not ratified the ERA. Many of our members are also active in other feminist organizations, such as WCML and NWSA, but programs and projects together with such organizations have so far come about through the initiative of individual members. In the future, we hope to make our presence felt internationally, through the IVG, and possibly through other organizations as well.

WiG's Influence on Our Field(s)

The influence of WiG on other associations and/ or in German Studies and the teaching of German is somewhat difficult to assess, but certain things can be established. For one, WiG's early efforts to expose the sexism in German textbooks and other teaching materials were not without consequences. Reviews were sent to publishers and textbook authors, workshops on sexism in teaching materials were arranged (e.g. AATG 1976, 1977) and textbook authors were invited to attend. Recent revisions and new editions of various textbooks reflect efforts to eliminate at least the most blatant examples of sexist practices -- though in some cases the changes are primarily superficial and sometimes inconsistent[4] Currently, WiG is involved in a "second wave" of text-

9

book reviewing; critiques of sexist content have been expanded and deepened to address other, related issues as well, such as racism, classism, heterosexism/homophobia, and so on.[5]

Another thing that can be clearly documented is that WiG sessions at MLA and AATG conventions are always well attended, indicating wide interest in our topics. (If attendance were the only criterion we could prove greater interest in our topics than in some of the traditional Germanistik-programs.) A positive development can be observed in scholarly journals as well: prior to 1976 there were virtually no articles published in our field that could by any stretch of the imagination be considered a contribution to feminist research. Since then, such articles have appeared with some regularity, though they are still scattered. For example, in the German Quarterly, which publishes 20-25 articles each year, we find six feminist contributions between 1977 and 1982. In the case of Unterrichtspraxis, we find one issue (No. 1, 1976) with a special section, "Focus on Women and Germanistik," then (only) six feminist contributions 1977-1982 (UP publishes 35-40 articles per year). An investigation of other journals in our field would probably turn up a similar pattern. By this measure, we have advanced from zero to tokenism; to look at it from a more positive angle, it is probable that these published contributions are only beginning to have any effect on the work of other scholars.

Concerning influence on the curriculum and the preparation of students, it would be useful to establish how many dissertations dealing with German women's literature and/or feminist approaches to German literature have been written since the early 1970s.[6] My preliminary investigation, based on the lists published annually in the Modern Language Journal (MLJ) yielded some suggestive results. I noted 81 dissertations in German and Comparative Literature completed between 1970 and 1981 that may, on the basis of their titles, be classified as research on women, broadly defined. Further work is necessary to establish how many of these represent a contribution to feminist research, since it is obviously impossible to tell from the title alone.

While this preliminary study does document a

considerable increase in the number of dissertations
that can be classified as research on women, espe -
cially since about 1973 (see appendix), it must also
be pointed out that 81 such studies still represent
a small proportion of all dissertations completed in
the fields of German Studies and Comparative Literature.[7] Also, the word "feminist" appears in only
one of the 81 titles -- in my opinion, unwelcome evidence that feminism is still considered dangerous
(e.g., by doctoral candidates, who fear, and not
without reason, that they won't easily find a job if
they are "labelled" as feminists), or "unscholarly"
(by graduate faculty). Certainly there are numerous
recent Ph.D's who could confirm both attitudes from
their own experience.

Other generalizations that can be made on the
basis of this preliminary investigation concern the
research subjects. In the appendix, I have arranged
the titles into two broad, partly overlapping categories: 1) German women authors/women's literature,
and 2) images of women, women's role, etc. The latter
category includes dissertations dealing with sex
roles, androgyny, female archetypes, and so on in
male-authored works as well as in works by women. We
can observe a drop in the number of "images of women"
studies after about 1977, which corresponds to the
increasing diversity of feminist approaches to literature during the mid-1970s and later. We can also
see that most of the studies of individual authors
(23 of the 81 titles) treat the better-known women
writers (Anna Seghers, Christa Wolf, Ingeborg
Bachmann, Else Lasker-Schüler, Annette von Drost-
Hülshoff) -- the ones who have already been allowed
to enter the German literary canon.[8]

Thus, this provisional investigation also suggests directions for much-needed changes. Women's
literature and feminist literary criticism still
need to be integrated into the curriculum of graduate
and undergraduate German departments; doctoral candidates cannot easily take feminist perspectives
into account in their dissertation research if they
have no background in feminist criticism or have
studied almost no women authors. It is not easy to
summarize an influence by WiG on the profession,
since our work cannot be entirely separated from the
Women's Studies movement or the women's movement
as a whole. Still, I believe our successes, especial-

ly at conferences, in the area of teaching materials, and in print, do indicate that our organization has contributed to a changing consciousness in the profession, and to the emergence of new research. After some eight years of effort, we are also in a better position to assess how to proceed from here.

Progress, Process and Contradictions

On the subject of material in print, a small number of special volumes published or initiated by our organization should also be mentioned. The 1977 Women in German conference remains the only one whose proceedings were published.[9] Besides this, there are two essay collections, Beyond the Eternal Feminine[10] and Gestaltet und Gestaltend,[11] and most recently, a collection of course syllabi.[12] The present volume is the first in a planned annual series, which is intended to provide a new outlet for papers related to German Studies and feminism, especially interdisciplinary and experimental work that couldn't readily be accomodated by traditional journals. If successful, this project should contribute to the expansion and redefinition of scholarly publication in our field. In the process, our organization will doubtless change somewhat also.

For good or ill, it is still true that our successes do change us even as we attempt to change institutions through our successes. By way of illustration, I will cite Jeannine Blackwell's commentary on our 1981 MLA session "German Women Writers of the Romantic Period," which surpassed even our own expectations:
> "It might just be the best WiG session we've
> ever had -- great papers on profound top-
> ics, constructive and uncatty commentary...
> and Ingeborg Drewitz and Gisela Dischner
> there as inspiration....But there were so
> many people there, sitting in neat rows,
> with a raised podium, that I had the
> uneasy feeling we were no longer the
> comfortable, down-home, frowsy, cheerfully
> disorganized small circle of friends that
> WiG used to be. And a good thing, too....
> Let's face it, we've gone big time...
> We have gained a lot, because they are
> listening to us now, but we are of neces-
> sity losing that sense of togetherness
> which those convention successes some-

times provided. Our very success in numbers makes the circle impossible."
(WiG Newsletter No. 27, Mar. 1982, p.3).

The circle referred to is, first, simply the circular seating arrangement, where everyone present can see everyone else. It is a supportive, affirming form which facilitates mutual sharing and process-oriented work. Beyond that, of course, it is the sense of shared commitment and goals. The loss of the first -- as Jeannine says, unavoidable when numbers pass a certain point -- should not necessarily lead to loss of the second; still, it is threatening. Recently, the contradictions surrounding success in numbers have been a major concern at the annual WiG conferences also.

Another "contradiction of success" has to do with the membership of WiG. The majority of our approximately 350 members are professors, roughly one third are students. In general, students have contributed, and continue to contribute a great deal to WiG: most members of the Madison newsletter collective mentioned above were students; students have organized or co-organized many conference sessions and workshops for WiG and/or presented papers (e.g., in the just-discussed Romanticism session, three of the seven papers presented were by students); there are numerous student contributions to the essay collections mentioned above, and so on. Thus, collaboration between students and professors is one of WiG's successes, and remains an important priority (as formulated by Patricia Herminghouse, "für den Nachwuchs sorgen."). Still, students and professors are Germanistinnen. And, as discussed earlier, our very name was chosen to suggest a wider membership. There is only a handful of high school German teachers among our members, and relatively few members come from other disciplines. The contradiction I see is that even as we come together to try to change our institutions, we are becoming a kind of institution ourselves. This is not only a problem for WiG; similar observations have been made about other feminist organizations. I quote one of the presenters at the 1982 NWSA convention:
"The women's movement has developed through a process of women coming from different places in the society, coming to have a voice, coming to develop new issues;

13

but there is a way in which our very
successes...create a kind of crystallization of what we come to see as the
issues, and a way in which they define the
participants, the people who are invited
to the movement, the people whose issues
are already there: the issues that are
made part of the academic work that we do,
part of our philosophical, theoretical
and political thinking. So that out of
this very process which is the success
of what we have done, there is also a
further silencing of those who have not
yet been invited and for whom this process
of crystallization closes off the possibility
of speaking....the ordinary institutions
in which we work do not...provide for the
presence and voices of those who are not
heard in this society...."[13]
It is clear, in my opinion, that WiG, like other feminist organizations, will have to grapple with the
problem of those who are silenced anew by our successes. How we can do so without totally exhausting
our energies remains to be seen.

Invisible Accomplishments

In closing, I wish to turn briefly to a very
positive aspect of WiG's work which I call our invisible accomplishments, and which I would like to make
more visible by naming and describing it. I mean the
work which is not defined as work by our institutions: the "housework" of WiG; the work of providing
emotional and professional support for one another;
the work of producing and reproducing relationships.

I believe that the work of providing support is
one of the most important things we do; certainly
this aspect of WiG was important for me personally.
I doubt that I would ever have ventured to "submit"
papers to conferences or write for publication if
I had not been asked, in 1976, to prepare a presentation on sexism in textbooks for a WiG session at
AATG. Through WiG, I was able to find a voice that
had eluded me before. I cannot say how many other
women feel as I do, but I suspect my experiences are
not unique in this regard. And even in less extreme
cases, mutual support can be decisive, especially
because of the isolation that many of us feel in our
departments, an isolation which may be suspended

14

only once a year, at the annual WiG conference.
It was not by accident that Sara Lennox, in 1982,
called the annual conference "eine konkrete Utopie."
It is our space, a place where, for a few days, we
can begin to come closer to realizing our visions,
to reflect on goals that reach beyond the ever-pres-
ent, day-to-day problems (How can I survive my tenure review/thesis defense/unemployment/battle with
hostile administrators who want to abolish Women's
Studies, etc.). The "utopian" aspect of the conferences will, again, mean different things to different women. For me, it means a supportive and stim-
ulating environment where I feel stronger, more
confident, even more "intelligent" than at other
times. Women taking each other seriously, caring
about each other, being ready to change if something
isn't working, and the often-mentioned attention to
process are all part of the "utopia." -- The work
of providing support is not, of course, restricted
to conferences but also takes place in private, where
it is even more invisible. It ranges from late-night
phone calls to discuss a personal crisis, to long
hours spent reviewing manuscripts for a WiG-col-
league's tenure or promotion case, to networking of
all kinds. The network is no less tangible for
being invisible.

The structure and "administration" of WiG is
another part of the invisible work -- the "housework"
of the organization. (In fact, it is even invisible
to some of our own members). Since its beginnings,
WiG has had a very loose structure; this is doubtless
related to trends in the American women's movement
at the time, which strongly leaned toward the abol-
ishment of all hierarchies, sometimes leading to
suspicion of any structure whatsoever.[14] Thus, WiG
has no "president," no "executive committee," etc.
Since 1977-78 there has been a steering committee
consisting of six women from various geographical
regions of the US serving staggered terms. The
roles of the committee and its members have been re-
defined or clarified several times in response to
the changing needs of the organization. The committee
is responsible for carrying out the ongoing work of
the organization, as agreed in the planning meeting
at each year's conference. Depending on the projects underway at any given time, this may require
a large investment of time and energy. Since none
of us is paid for her work, this system relies

15

on the willingness of individuals to make WiG a priority -- not an easy decision when the work to be done isn't recognized as work by those outside our organization.

This relatively "structureless" structure has the advantage that there are no "channels" of authority to pass through; major decisions are the result of group process, and in principle, all members can feel free to propose projects to the group, volunteer to lead projects or decline to do so, and so on. However, there are also disadvantages. For example, despite the (aimed-for) absence of hierarchy, it can be difficult for new members to assert themselves in the group, and women who have been active members for several years may be seen as tone-setting even if they actively seek to avoid this role. Collective, democratic processes and procedures must continually be recreated; each conference presents a new situation in terms of group dynamics and in terms of which concerns are seen as most pressing.

A last category of invisible accomplishments has to do with friendships that develop within the group. Through WiG we find friends with whom we can talk about all aspects of our lives, our "real" (paid) work as well as the "work" of our personal lives; our love-relationships, our children; a birth, an abortion; we can admit that the reason why we didn't meet a deadline is for "personal" reasons. We don't have to pretend that these various parts of our lives are separate, but can let them come together very concretely, even if only temporarily. At our conferences, we also celebrate together, making time for fun, dancing, gossip, even (dare we admit this in print?) frivolity. Recreation becomes re-creation. Aspiring to a feminist way of being together creates space in which, at least briefly, the contradictions and fragmentation are suspended.

Looking Toward the Future ...

The contradictions in which we work (must work) appear already in our name, Women in German, and constitute a dynamic tension apparent in all the projects and activities of our organization: in the format and interaction patterns of our conferences; in the choice of topics for conferences and workshops; in the choice of the language used in discus-

16

sions; in work with other associations and with the universities, publishers and other institutions we work in, or on whose margins we work; in the structure of our organization. Both our concrete, visible accomplishments and the utopian moments must be kept in mind if our goal of radically transforming scholarship and teaching in our field is to be achieved.

Indiana U.- Purdue U.
at Fort Wayne

Notes

* This paper is based on a presentation entitled "Sieben Jahre Women in German: An- und Widersprüche einer feministischen Germanistik," presented at the conference "Feministische Literaturwissenschaft: Zum Verhältnis von Frauenbildern und Frauenliteratur," Hamburg, May 1983. The German version of the paper is published in the conference proceedings (Argument, 1984).

[1] NWSA Constitution, Women's Studies Quarterly, Vol. X, No. 4 (Winter 1982), p. 41.

[2] At one time, certain men objected to the name, since they felt excluded by it, sigh. See WiG Newsletter No. 8 (Sept. 1976), p. 3. WiG has neither sought to recruit male members nor turned away those who were prepared to take our work seriously. For some years there was a male member of the Madison collective, and (a few) men have attended the annual WiG conferences. This fact led, in 1978, to the establishment of a policy to hold one "women only" session at each year's conference.

[3] The current address of the WiG newsletter is: Women in German, Dept. of Modern Foreign Languages, Indiana U.-Purdue U., Fort Wayne, IN 46805.

[4] See Jeanette Clausen, "Textbooks and (In-)-Equality: A Survey of Literary Readers for Elementary and Intermediate German," Unterrichtspraxis Vol. 15, No. 2 (Fall 1982), pp. 244-253.

[5] A new collection of textbook reviews, edited

by Linda Schelbitzki Pickle, appeared in April 1983. The reviews concentrated on some of the most frequently used German textbooks for the elementary and intermediate levels. Copies of the reviews went to the textbook authors and to the publishers, as well as to all WiG members. Also on the subject of teaching materials, see: Barbara D. Wright, "Mainstreaming the FL Curriculum: Female and Male Stereotyping in Beginning-Level Teaching Materials," (Conference Report), WiG Newsletter No. 30 (Mar. 1983), pp. 7-10.

[6] The date relates to the emergence of the first Women's Studies programs in the U.S. See Florence Howe, Seven Years Later (Old Westbury, NY: The Feminist Press, 1977).

[7] According to a recent survey, there were 74 dissertations in German and Comparative Literature completed during only one year. See David P. Benseler, "A Survey of US Doctoral Degrees Related to the Teaching of German--1981," UP, Vol. 15, No. 2 (1982), pp. 270-273.

[8] See Jeannine Blackwell, "Deconstructing the Canon," presented at the MLA Annual Meeting, December 1983.

[9] Proceedings of the Second Annual Women in German Symposium, ed. Kay Goodman and Ruth H. Sanders (Oxford, Ohio: Miami University, Sept. 1977). After 1977, conference organizers discouraged the presentation of finished papers in favor of thesis-like working papers; these, of course, are less suited for publication.

[10] Beyond the Eternal Feminine: Critical Essays on Women and German Literature, ed. Susan L. Cocalis and Kay Goodman (Stuttgart: Akademischer Verlag Hans-Dieter Heinz, 1982). This project, begun in 1977, was intended as a kind of WiG yearbook; however, publication was delayed for several years because of difficulties in finding a publisher.

[11] Gestaltet und Gestaltend: Frauen in der deutschen Literatur, ed. Marianne Burkhard. (Amsterdamer Beiträge zur neueren Germanistik, Vol. 10, 1980.) This project was initiated by Marianne Burkhard and the editors of ABnG.

18

[12] German Studies and Women's Studies: New Directions in Literary and Interdisciplinary Course Approaches, ed. Sidonie Cassirer and Sydna Stern Weiss, 1983. Supported by grants from Hamilton College and the Kirkland Endowment. Available from: Women in German, Dept. of Modern Foreign Languages, Indiana U.-Purdue U., Fort Wayne, IN 46805.

[13] "Highlights of the 1982 NWSA Convention. Excerpts from the Opening Plenary Session 'Feminist Scholarship and Feminist Connection,'" Women's Studies Quarterly, Vol. X, No. 3 (Fall 1982), pp. 5-8.

[14] On the "ideology of structurelessness," cf. Jo Freeman, "The Women's Liberation Movement: Its Origins, Structures, Impact, and Ideas," in Women: A Feminist Perspective, ed. Jo Freeman (Palo Alto, CA: Mayfield Publ. Co., 1975), pp. 448-460.

Appendix

U.S. Doctoral Dissertations Related to Research on Women and General Literature, 1970-1981.

The sources for this listing are the lists of dissertations published annually by the Modern Language Journal, Vol. 55, No. 1 (January 1971) through Vol. 66, No. 3 (Fall 1982). These lists are published by MLJ on the basis of information provided by the degree-granting institutions. Thus, the list is not necessarily complete and there may be some errors, or entries may differ in certain details from those appearing in DAI. Hence, this list should be used with caution; it is offered only as a first approximation of an overview in this area.

The lists provided here follow the listing practice used in the respective MLJ volumes, by calendar year since 1980, by academic year for earlier volumes. The studies were grouped into two broad categories, (A) German Women Writers/Women's Literature and (B) Images of Women/Women's Role, etc. on the basis of their titles. These categories are not intended to imply any assessment of the content.

Calendar Year 1981

A. German Women Writers/Women's Literature

Heinemann, Marlene E. Women Prose Writers of the Nazi Holocaust. (Indiana U., H.Remak).

Kaleyias, George P. Reflections of History: The Stories of Anna Seghers in Weimar Germany and in Exile (1924-47). (U. of Maryland, Peter Beiken).

Kingsbury, Victoria. The Writing of Christa Wolf: From Objective to Subjective Authenticity. (Michigan State U., Thomas H. Falk).

Koester, Diane. Techniques of Character Portrayal in the German Novel of the Eighteenth Century: Schnabel, von Loen, Gellert, Wieland, La Roche. (Johns Hopkins, L.E. Kurth).

Schleimer, Gloria. Protected Self-Revelation: A Study of the Works of Four Nineteenth-Century Women Poets, Marceline Desbordes-Valmore, Annette von Droste-Hülshoff, Elizabeth Barrett-Browning and Emily Brontë. (U. Cal., Irvine, Renée Hubert).

Stuecher, Dorothea D. Double Jeopardy: Nineteenth Century German-American Women Writers. (U. Minnesota, Ruth-Ellen B. Joeres).

Weingant, Liselotte. Das Bild des Mannes im Frauenroman der siebziger Jahre. (U. Illinois, Walter Höllerer).

B.   Images of Women/Women's Role, etc.

Borisoff, Deborah J. Changing Aspects in 20th Century Faustian Works: The Woman as Illuminator and Liberator of the Isolated Hero. (New York U., Doris Guilloton).

Ritter, Liselotte T. Das Potential der Frau bei Heinrich von Kleist. (Michigan State U., Raimund Belgardt).

Rowe, Marianne L. A Typology of Women Characters in the German Naturalist Novel. (Rice U., Michael Winkler).

Zak, Nancy. The Portrayal of the Heroine in Chrétien de Troy's Erec et Enide, Gottfried von Strassburg's Tristan, and Flamenca. (U. Cal., Berkeley, Joseph Duggan).

Fall 1979-Calendar Year 1980

A. German Women Writers/Women's Literature

Aydelott, Helen E. Didacticism in Eighteenth Century Prose Fiction: Studies in Richardson, Fielding, Diderot and La Roche. (Indiana U., Peter Boerner, Merritt Lawlis).

Blumberg, Sigrid J. Die Ballade als künstlerische Notwendigkeit im 19. Jahrhundert (Droste, Hebbel, Meyer, Fontane). (U. Cal., Davis, Clifford Bernd).

Snapper, Gerda H. Entfremdung und Isolation in den Prosawerken von Marie von Ebner-Eschenbach. (U. Cal., Berkeley, Marianne Bonwit).

Sull, Young-Suk. Die Lyrik Else Lasker-Schülers. Stilelemente und Themenkreise. (George Washington U., Klaus Thoenelt).

Toegl, Edith. Emily Dickinson and Annette von Droste-Hülshoff: Poets as Women. (Washington, Diana I. Behler).

Zimmerman, Inge M. Der Mensch im Spiegel des Tierbildes: Untersuchungen zum Werk Else Lasker-Schülers. (U. Kansas, Warren Maurer).

B. Images of Women/Women's Role, etc.

Beck, Hamilton H. Hippel and the Eighteenth-Century Novel. (Cornell, Sander Gilman).

Friedrichsmeyer, Sara. The Androgynous Ideal and Its Resurgence in the Works of Novalis and Friedrich Schlegel. (U. Cincinnati, Helga Slessarev).

Prandi, Julie. Spirited Women Heroes of the Goethezeit: Women Protagonists in the Dramas of Goethe, Schiller and Kleist. (U. Cal., Berkeley, Bluma Goldstein).

Tubach, Sally P. Female Homoeroticism in German Literature. (U. Cal., Berkeley, Winfried Kudszus).

1978-79

A. German Women Writers/Women's Literature

21

Dedner, Doris Smith. From Infanticide to Single Motherhood: The Evolution of a Literary Theme in the Works of Clara Viebig. (Indiana U., H. Remak).

Gutzmann, Gertraud G. Schriftsteller und Literatur: Ihre gesellschaftliche Funktion im Werk von Anna Seghers. (U. Mass., Wilfried Malsch).

Hoffmeister, Donna L. Strategies and Counter-Strategies: Dramatic Dialogue in the Milieu Plays of Marieluise Fleisser and Franz Xaver Kroetz. (Brown U., Karl S. Weimar).

Levin, Tobe J. Ideology and Aesthetics in German Neo-Feminist Fiction: Verena Stefan, Elfriede Jelinek, Margot Schroeder. (Cornell, Inta Ezergailis).

Schulz, Beate A. Struktur- und Motivanalyse ausgewählter Prosa von Ingeborg Bachmann. (U. Maryland, Otto F. Best).

B.   Images of Women/Women's Role, etc.

Franke, Elke K. The Role of Women in Dürrenmatt's Plays. (Rochester, Paul Hernadi).

McCullar, Sylvia Y. "Ideal" versus "Real": Womanhood as Portrayed in the Literature and Correspondence of Early German Romanticism (Rice U., Margret Eifler).

Stiewe, Gerhild E. Die Rolle der Frau in der DDR Literatur.(U. Minnesota, Frank Hirschbach).

1977-78

A.   German Women Writers/Women's Literature

Carpenter, Victor W. A Study of Clara Viebig's Novellen. (Pennsylvania, Frank Trommler).

Holt, Lynne, W. The Relationship of Silence and Music to Language in Ingeborg Bachmann's Poetry. (Harvard, Henry Hatfield).

Wichmann, Brigitte M. From Sex-Role Identification toward Androgyny: A Study of Major Works of Simone de Beauvoir, Doris Lessing and Christa Wolf. (Purdue, Margaret Church).

B. Images of Women/Women's Roles

Ambrose, Mary Jo V. An Examination of the Independent Role of Women in Friedrich Hebbel's Major Dramas. (Pennsylvania, André von Gronicka).

Kienbaum, Barbara E. Die Frauengestalten in Theodor Fontanes Berliner Romanen. (Michigan State U., Mark Kistler).

Mittelmann, Hanni. Die Utopie des weiblichen Glücks in den Romanen Theodor Fontanes. (UCLA, Erhard Bahr).

Tally, Frances M. From the Mystery of Conception to the Miracle of Birth: An Historical Survey of Beliefs and Rituals surrounding the Pregnant Woman in Germanic Folk Tradition, Including Modern America. (UCLA, Wayland Hand).

1976-77

A. German Women Writers/Women's Literature

Crews, Elizabeth T. Wort und Wahrheit. Das Problem der Sprache in der Prosa Ingeborg Bachmanns. (Minnesota, Wolfgang Taraba).

Goodman, Katherine R. German Women and Autobiography in the Nineteenth Century: Luise Aston, Fanny Lewald, Malwida von Meysenbug and Marie von Ebner-Esenbach. (Wisconsin, Reinhold Grimm).

Isajiw, Oksana. The Idea of Self-Realization in the Works of Anna Seghers. (Pennsylvania, Frank Trommler).

Kraft, Kent T. The Eye Sees More Than the Heart Knows: The Visionary Cosmology of Hildegard of Bingen. (Wisconsin, Fannie Le Moene).

Morse, Margaret. Motifs of Women in the Works of Selected Women Writers of the Nineteenth and Twentieth Centuries. (U. Cal., Berkeley, Winfried Kudszus).

Stern, Dagmar C. Hilde Domin: From Exile to Ideal. (Indiana, Louis Helbig).

B.   Images of Women/Women's Role,etc.

Balinkin, Ausma. The Central Women Figures in
Zuckmayer's Dramas. (Cincinnati, Guy Stern).

Heather, Barbara S. Die Frau in Gottfried Benns
Werk: Bild und Funktion. (Washington, William Rey).

Herrera, Bertilia. Racine, Alfieri and Schiller:
A Comparative Study of Heroines. (U. Cal., River-
side, Jean-Pierre Barricelli).

Lakin, Michael J. Angela and Lucrezia in C.F.
Meyer's Angela Borgia. (SUNY Buffalo, Erika
Metzger).

Nussbaum, Laureen. The Image of Women in the
Work of Bertolt Brecht. (Washington, Sammy McLean).

Place, Mary E. The Characterization of Women in
the Plays of Frank Wedekind. (Vanderbilt, Josef
Rysan).

Whelan, Dolores H. Das Bild der Frau in den
Komödien Eduard von Bauernfelds 1830-1870. (Connecticut, George Reinhardt).

1975-76

A.   German Women Writers/Women's Literature

Cervantes, Eleonore K. Strukturbezüge in der
Lyrik von Nelly Sachs: Eine Textanalyse des
Zyklus Die Suchende im Bezug zum Lyrischen
Gesamtwerk. (Oregon, Peter Gontrum).

B.   Images of Women/Women's Role, etc.

Darmon, Nicole M.S. Frauen und Erotik in Otto
Flakes Romanwerk. (Pennsylvania, Heinz Moenken-
meyer).

Grayson, Patricia J. Fathers and Daughters in
German Drama. (Pennsylvania, Heinz Monkenmeyer).

Harrison, James W. Melusine: Matriarch, Elemental
Spirit, Archetype. (N. Carolina, Ria Stambaugh).

Kuplis, Aija. The Image of Woman in Bertolt

Brecht's Poetry. (Wisconsin, Reinhold Grimm).

Langerova, Vera Z. Women Characters in the Works of Uwe Johnson. (Vanderbilt, Phillip H. Rhein).

Rodner, Felicity A. Women in Gotthelf's Short Stories. (Harvard, Jack Stein).

Rose, Ingrid B. Social Stereotypes and Female Actualities. A Dimension of Social Criticism in Selected Works by Fontane, Hauptmann, Wedekind and Schnitzler. (Princeton, Theodore Ziolkowski).

Ward, Dorothy Cox. The Two Marys: A Study of the Women in Herman Hesse's Fiction. (Columbia, Joseph Bauke).

1974-75

A. German Women Writers/Women's Literature

Handels, Nancy F. Catharina Regina von Greiffenbergs Lieder und Sonette: Das Problem von Dichtung und Mystik. (Stanford, Kurt Mueller-Vollmer).

Summerfield, Ellen B. Die Auflösung der Figur in Ingeborg Bachmanns Roman Malina. (Connecticut, Hildegard Emmel).

B. Images of Women/Women's Role, etc.

Drost, Carla L. The Major Female Characters in the Dramas of Georg Büchner. (Louisiana State, Edward Newby).

Leheis, Jutta S. Zauber des Evatums: Zur Frauenfrage bei Theodor Fontane. (U. Mass., Sigrid Bauschinger).

Teuschner, Gerhart. Women in Grimmelshausen's Wunderbarliches Vogelnest, Parts I and II. (SUNY Buffalo, A. George de Capua).

1973-74

A. German Women Writers/ Women's Literature

Fleming, Mariana M. Ilse Aichinger: Die Sicht der Entfremdung -- Ein Versuch, die Symbolik ihres

Werkes von dessen Gesamtstruktur her zu erschliessen. (Maryland, Otto Best).

Gooday, Frances A. Mechthild von Magdeburg and Hadwich of Antwerp: A Comparison. (Harvard, Eckehard Simon).

Lee, Eve. The Idea of Humanity in the Short Stories of Luise Rinser. (Vanderbilt, Phillip H. Rhein).

Pomps, Helga. Christa Wolf: Nachdenken über Christa T. A Study in Human Development. (Colorado, Wesley V. Blomster).

Siekhaus, Elisabeth B. Die lyrischen Sonette der Catharina Regina von Greiffenberg. (U. Cal., Berkeley, Blake E. Spahr).

B. Images of Women/Women's Role, etc.

Casey, Paul. Susanna in German Literature. Theme and Variations. (Johns Hopkins, Liselotte Kurth).

Hove, David A. Lessing's Heroines and their Literary Models. (Iowa, Edward Dvoretzky).

Luciano, David R. The Proto-Indo-European Concept of Women: A Study in Comparative Philology, Anthropology, and Comparative Religion. (Connecticut, Terrence McCormick).

Schmitt, Willa E. The Changing Role of Women in the Works of Arthur Schnitzler. (Wisconsin, Ian Loram).

Zivers, Isolde M. "Undine": Tradition and Interpretation of an Archetypal Figure in German Literature. (Rutgers, John Fitzell).

1972-73

A. German Women Writers

Liefle, Helmut W. Sybille Schwarz (1621-1638): Leben und Werk. (Illinois, Henri Stegemeier).

1971-72

A. German Women Writers

Dodds, Dinah J. Sachs, Schoenberg: A Study on Myth in Word and Music. (Colorado, Wesley V. Blomster).

Franklin, James Clair. Love and Transition: Water and the Imagery of Liquids in the Work of Mechthild von Magdeburg. (Case Western Reserve, Ruth Angress).

1970-71

A. German Women Writers/Women's Literature

Novak, Sigrid. Images of Womanhood in the Works of German Female Dramatists. (Johns Hopkins, William H. McClain).

Slocum, Malve Kristin. Untersuchungen zu Lob und Spiel in den "Sonetten" der Katharina Regina von Greiffenberg. (Cornell, H. Deinert).

B. Images of Women/Women's Role, etc.

Cantwell, Joan. The Role of the Woman in the Works of Odon von Horvath. (Wisconsin, Ian Loram).

Joeres, Ruth-Ellen. Wally the Skeptic: Translation and Commentary. (Johns Hopkins, William H. McClain).

1969-70

B. Images of Women/Women's Roles, etc.

Baillet, Theresia M. Die dichterischen Gestaltungen der heidnischen und christlichen Frau im Werk Eichendorffs. (Washington)

Ezergailis, Inta Miske. An Ambiguous Dialectic: The Female Principle in Thomas Mann's Work. (Cornell).

Sigrid Weigel

Das Schreiben des Mangels als Produktion
von Utopie

I

Die Vermittlung zwischen Feminismus und Literaturwissenschaft ist in der BRD noch recht unterent-
wickelt. Wenn auch ein weitgehendes Einverständnis
über die Fragestellungen und über die Notwendigkeit
neuer, eigener Methoden besteht,[1] so ist deren Aus-
arbeitung und Praktizierung noch nicht sehr weit ge-
diehen. Dies gilt mehr noch für die Erforschung von
Frauenbildern und Weiblichkeitsmustern in der Philo-
sophie und Literatur von Männern, für die ja mit der
ideolokritischen Studie Silvia Bovenschens[2] und der
sozialpsychologischen Klaus Theweleits[3] zwei umfang-
reiche Untersuchungen vorliegen. Deren Perspektiven
wurden in vielen Einzeluntersuchungen seither fort-
gesetzt und modifiziert.

Im Bemühen um eine Rekonstruktion weiblicher literarischer Tradition aber stehen historische Forschung
und theoretische Überlegungen über weibliche Sprache
und Schrift oft weit auseinander:

--Häufig überwiegt das Interesse an der Biographie der Autorin dasjenige an ihren Texten.[4]

--Bei der Interpretation von Frauenliteratur werden oft nur die expliziten Äusserungen zur
Frauenemanzipation, nicht aber widersprüchliche
Momente, Erzählmuster und Schreibstrategien
untersucht.[5]

Anregungen für die Analyse des Phänomens, dass man bei
der Lektüre von Frauenliteratur auf viele Frauenbilder
und Stereotypen trifft, die aus der männlichen Literatur bekannt sind, kommen aus dem Ausland. So etwa
von S. Gubar/S. Gilberts Darstellung The Madwoman in
the Attic[6] und von der Zusammenstellung amerikanischer,
englischer und französischer Beiträge unter dem Titel
Listen der Ohnmacht von C. Honnegger/B. Heintz.[7]

Der Grund für diese Situation liegt darin, dass
die Interpretation konkreter Texte in der theoretisch-
en Diskussion der BRD eine viel zu geringe Rolle
spielt. So sind die in den Untersuchungen zur Kultur-

29

geschichte des Weiblichen gewonnenen Erkenntnisse über
den Ort der Frau in der männlichen Ordnung noch kaum
für die Deutung literarischer Artikulationen von Frauen
genutzt. So werden die in diesen Untersuchungen ver-
wendeten Topoi (wie z.B. der von der "Geschichtslosig-
keit der Frau," von der Existenz der Frau an den "Rän-
dern" des Patriarchats, von der Funktion der Frauenbilder als "Spiegel" ihrer männlichen Produzenten,
auch die Bestimmung des Weiblichen als "Mangel" bzw.
"Negation") bislang weitgehend metaphorisch oder sym-
bolisch benutzt, ohne dass sie für die Textinterpre-
tation fruchtbar gemacht werden.

Aus dieser Beobachtung ergibt sich für mich die
Notwendigkeit und Relevanz feministischer Literatur-
kritik, aus ihr begründet sich auch mein methodischer
Ausgangspunkt, die zitierten Topoi in der Interpretation von Texten anzuwenden und damit weibliche
Schreibpraxis als Ausdrucksformen von Frauen unter
Bedingungen und in den Strukturen einer männlichen
Ordnung zu untersuchen. Häufig wird die Frage nach
den Besonderheiten "weiblichen Schreibens" ahistorisch
gestellt, vor allem im Kontext der Rezeption der französischen Strukturalistinnen in der BRD und in den
Gruppen "schreibender Frauen". Deshalb gehe ich von
einer Unterscheidung der ideologischen, empirischen
und utopischen Bedeutung des Begriffes "weiblich"
aus und trenne strikt zwischen Texten von Männern und
Frauen.

Populärer und verbreiteter als die Entwicklung
feministischer Literaturkritik im engeren Sinne[8] sind
in letzter Zeit kunst- und kulturgeschichtliche Arbeiten über Mythos und Matriarchat. Während die Bemühung-
en, die unter dem Thema "Mythos Frau" stehen,[9] z.T.
die verborgene weibliche Realität und Produktivität
in den Bildern aufspüren und die patriarchalischen
Strukturen in den Überlieferungen aufdecken wollen,[10]
sind die Arbeiten über matriarchalische Vorgeschichte
eher auf der Suche nach einem historischen Vorbild,
das als Folie für weibliche Utopie gelten kann. Be-
sonders in den Arbeiten von H. Göttner-Abendroth[11]
wird eine solche problematische Gleichsetzung von
Mythos, realer Vorgeschichte und Utopie vorgenommen.

II

Methodischer Ausgangspunkt für die Untersuchung weiblicher Schreibpraxis[12] ist für mich, dass die Frau in der männlichen Ordnung als "anderes Geschlecht" (Beauvoir) existiert, dass sie beteiligt und ausgegrenzt zugleich ist. Dabei ist ihre Selbstbetrachtung durch Spiegelbilder verstellt, die sie als untergeordnetes, unvollkommenes oder aber als entrücktes, überhöhtes Naturwesen zeichnen. In der Literatur von Frauen drückt sich dies als Problem der Wahrnehmungs- und Erzählperspektive aus.

Die Geschichte der Frauenliteratur lässt sich als permanente, notwendige Befreiung des Schreibens aus männlicher Perspektive hin zu einer autonomen weiblichen Schreibweise beschreiben. Dabei verstehe ich diese Bewegung nicht als phasenweise, wie E. Showalter in ihrer Einteilung in die feminine, feministische und female Phase,[13] oder als historische Chronologie, sondern untersuche sie in jedem einzelnen Text. Auf diese Weise lässt sich die auffällige Ambivalenz oder Widerspruchstruktur in sprachlichen Ausdrucksformen von Frauen begreifen. Kein Text, den eine Frau geschrieben hat, die im Patriarchat lebt, ist Ausdruck blosser Projektion. Auch der reine Entwurf von Befreiung kann darin nicht entwickelt sein. Vielmehr enthält die Literatur von Frauen jeweils unterschiedliche Schreibweisen der Doppelexistenz: des Lebens im Muster der herrschenden Frauenbilder und in der Antizipation der befreiten Frau.

Deshalb müssen Sprache und Schrift von Frauen daraufhin befragt werden, ob und wie sie mit dieser Doppelexistenz umgehen, ob sie sie nach einer Seite hin harmonisieren oder ob sie sie zum Sprechen bringen, d.h. wie sie den Raum im "nicht mehr" und "noch nicht" (Kristeva) füllen. Unter dieser Fragestellung habe ich in der Literatur von Frauen verschiedene Strategien festgestellt: Anpassung, Maskierungen und Verschlüsselungen, Versuche voluntaristischer Vervollkommung und utopischer Überschreitung des Mangels. Es gibt aber auch Strategien der schreibenden Gestaltung des Mangels, des Hindurchgehens durch die vorhandenen Frauenbilder bis zu ihrer Zerstörung. Und es gibt Strategien der Verabschiedung oder Entzauberung der Bilder und der Trauerarbeit daran.

31

III

Die Geschichte der Frauenliteratur beginnt in der zweiten Hälfte des 18. Jh., seit Schriftstellerinnen keine Einzelerscheinungen mehr sind und vermehrt weibliche Erfahrungen thematisieren. Seither stehen viele schreibende Frauen vor der Entscheidung zwischen ihrer eigenen Emanzipation oder der ihrer Heldin. Die Initiation einer Autorin in die Spielregeln kultureller Ordnung, ihr Durchbrechen weiblicher Rollenmuster, wird oft mit der Anpassung ihrer imaginierten Frauenfiguren bezahlt (vgl. das Fräulein von Sternheim von Sophie von La Roche). Andere Frauen verzichten darauf, zu veröffentlichen, weil sie sich nicht verstellen wollen (z.B. Rahel v. Varnhagen, Caroline Schlegel). Wieder andere veröffentlichen anonym oder unter einem männlichen Pseudonym, um nicht selbst für die Öffentlichkeit erkennbar aus der weiblichen Rolle zu fallen.

Im Entwurf eines männlichen Helden (z.B. in Blütenalter der Empfindung von Sophie Mereau) oder in der Gestaltung einer männlichen Erzählperspektive (z.B. in Indiana von George Sand) maskieren und verstellen Autorinnen ihre eigenen Erfahrungen und Wünsche, d.h. sie veröffentlichen sie nicht als genuin weibliche. Eine solche Geschlechtsumwandlung im Schreibakt wirkt sich auf die Fabel, auf die Charakterisierung der Figuren und selbst auf syntaktische Strukturen aus. Sehr spät erst wird eine, auch formal gestaltete, erkennbare Beziehung zwischen Autorin, Erzählerin und weiblicher Hauptperson gewagt. Erst dann ist literarisch eine umfassende weibliche Perspektive als Raum zur Entfaltung weiblicher Erfahrung und Geschichte geschaffen. Nicht immer aber ist es blosse Maskierung, wenn Frauen in die Männerrolle schlüpfen. Es kann auch Ausdruck der Sehnsucht nach Vollkommenheit sein. Für die Autorin, die darunter leidet, nur Frau und anders zu sein, kann die Erfüllung männlicher ästhetischer Normen und Muster als Ausweg aus ihrer Uneigentlichkeit erscheinen (vgl. Caroline von Günderrode).

Konventionelle Genres, von männlichen Autoren für ihre Bedürfnisse entwickelt, enthalten vielfach Erzählstrukturen und poetische Gesetzmässigkeiten, die die Bearbeitung weiblicher Erfahrung erschweren, weil sie die Zeit-, Raum- und Bedeutungshierarchien der männlichen Ordnung nachahmen. Eigenes Begehren und Aufbruchsmomente weiblicher Verfasser, die sich solcher Genres bedienen, sind häufig im Text verborgen. So stehen z.B. Ausbruchsphantasien der Heldin und eine

den geltenden Weiblichkeitsmustern entsprechende Fabel-
entwicklung (Entsagung) manchmal im krassen Widerspruch
zueinander (vgl. das Frühwerk Fanny Lewalds, einige
Romane Luise Mühlbachs). Dies ist u.a. eine Konse-
quenz der Fesselung weiblicher Phantasie, die aufgrund
ihrer Domestizierung nicht in Auseinandersetzung mit
sozialer Realität treten kann. Dadurch wird die Entwicklung konkreter Utopie bei Frauen behindert.

In paradoxer Verwendung konventioneller Genres
haben Frauen z.T. literarische Möglichkeiten gefunden,
um die Diskrepanz zwischen der Struktur ihrer Erfahr-
ung/Identitätssuche und den Strukturen männlicher
Poesie, wie z.B. Geschlossenheit, Kontinuität, Entwicklung, zu gestalten und zu bearbeiten. (Vg. Inga
Buhmanns Ich habe mir eine Geschichte geschrieben,
Christa Wolfs Kindheitsmuster).

Was von der herrschenden Literaturkritik in den
Texten von Schriftstellerinnen als Stilbruch oder als
Beleg für die Inferiorität weiblicher Poesie qualifi-
ziert wird, ist häufig Ausdruck der zum Sprechen ge-
brachten Doppelexistenz. Beispiele dafür sind die
gebrochene bzw. paradoxe Verwendung konventioneller
Genres oder die Gestaltung des gespaltenen Frauenbildes, das als Gefängnis weiblicher Lebensmöglich-
keiten erfahren wird. Das Leben im Zauber eines
herrschenden Frauenbildes, z.B. dem der "hohen Frau",
und Erfahrungen als Objekt der gewaltsamen Begierde
männlicher Sexualität, ausgedrückt in einem Text einer
Autorin, verlangt die Darstellung sehr verschiedener
"Realitäten". Dadurch entsteht eine Disharmonie im
Text, die aus der Präsenz entgegengesetzter Bedeutung-
en, Räume, atmosphärischer Eindrücke und Erlebnisse
resultiert. Solche Disharmonien sind notwendige Stil-
brüche, weil sie sprachliche Ausdrucksformen sind von
doppelten, verrückten oder gespaltenen Selbstbildern
ihrer Verfasserinnen (vgl. Louise Astons Aus dem Leben
einer Frau).

Der Entwurf einer neuen, emanzipierten bzw. befreiten Frau wird möglich erst über die Entzauberung
bzw. Zerstörung der herrschenden Frauenbilder. So wie
die Konstituierung der männlichen Ordnung sich dem
Ausschluss der Frauen verdankt und die männliche Kunst-
produktion der (Ab)Tötung bzw. Opferung des Weiblich-
en,[14] so ist umgekehrt für Schriftstellerinnen die
Zerstörung des Frauenbildes und der damit verbundenen
sprachlichen Strukturen, teils auch die symbolische

Tötung vom Schöpfer des Bildes, ein Schritt, der ihnen die Befreiung erst ermöglicht. Er macht sie frei für den Entwurf eines neuen Frauenbildes (vgl. Louise Astons Roman Lydia).

Durch die Zerstörung der Frauenbilder wird der Mangel eines eigenen Entwurfes erst zum Vorschein gebracht, wird die Uneigentlichkeit aller Bestimmungen des Weibes--als Imaginationen, Projektionen oder Phantasien männlicher Urheber--erst aufgedeckt. Die schreibende Hervorbringung des Mangels bzw. der Negation ist als Entschleierung für Frauen produktiv. Sie kann in fiktionalen Texten experimentell erprobt werden. Authentische Texte--vor allem Krankheitsberichte oder -tagebücher von Frauen--zeichnen im Medium der Sprache die Zerstörung des Bildes nach, die die Sprache der "Krankheit" am Körper der Autorin vorab schon betrieben hat (vgl. Texte magersüchtiger oder depressiver Frauen).

Die Entzauberung der Bilder ist häufig das Resultat einer--gelebten oder imaginierten--Durchquerung der Bilder. Da die Frau das "Weibliche" verkörpert, trägt sie das, was im Diskurs als Mangel definiert ist, in sich. Sie braucht daher nicht, wie Irigaray postuliert, die männlichen Diskurse zu durchqueren.[15] Die schreibende Bearbeitung der Bilder in ihr, die Durchquerung internalisierter Trugbilder und regressiven Begehrens, ist ein Stück Befreiung des "Weiblichen" in seiner utopischen Bedeutung. Befreiung wird erzielt nicht in der Form einer Setzung, sondern als Arbeit, indem die Schichten und Ablagerungen patriarchalischer Geschichte abgetragen werden.

Frauen, die im Schreiben das Verdrängte hervortreten lassen, finden nicht schon darin ein positives Programm, wie Cixous meint.[16] Sie stossen vielmehr auf die Fülle der Bilder in sich, auf den Wunsch nach Hingabe und Abhängigkeit ebenso wie auf Unabhängigkeits- und Befreiungsverlangen. In der Kommunikation mit anderen Frauen, d.h. im Austausch unterschiedlicher weiblicher Erfahrung, oder in der literarischen Verdoppelung, z.B. in verschiedenen Figuren oder im Blick der Erzählerin auf eine Figur, sind unterschiedliche Strategien der "sich selbst verdoppelnden Frau" (E. Lenk) zu sehen, in denen die "nicht mehr" gewünschten Bilder von den "noch nicht" erreichten Utopien unterschieden werden können. Diese Unterscheidung herauszuarbeiten, ist eine der wichtigsten und zugleich schwierigsten Aufgaben von Frauenliteratur.

IV

Eine komplexe und differenzierte Form der Gestaltung weiblicher Identitätsproblematik hat Ingeborg Bachmann in dem Roman Malina gefunden. Das 'Ich,' welches mit Ivan das Bild der hingebungsvollen Geliebten durchlebt, zum Überleben aber schliesslich der männlichen Vernunft Malinas die Regie über/in sich überlässt, kann schliesslich nur noch verschwinden. Die vielfältigen Todesarten des "Ich" hinterlassen einen Mangel: nämlich eine Frau, die mit ihrem "eigenen Ich" siegen kann. Mit dieser literarischen Hervorbringung des Mangels hat Ingeborg Bachmann eine Möglichkeit gefunden, trotz ihres Ungenügens an der-- männlichen und weiblichen--Sprache das "unbeschriebene Blatt" zu produzieren.

". . . und unsere Begeisterung für bestimmte herrliche Texte ist eigentlich die Begeisterung für das weisse, unbeschriebene Blatt, auf dem das noch Hinzuzugewinnende auch eingetragen scheint."17 Das "Hinzuzugewinnende" ist die positive Formulierung für Mangel. Diese These Ingeborg Bachmanns über Utopie, die in der poetischen Konkretisierung ihrer eigenen Prosa später geschlechtsspezifisch differenziert wird, deckt sich mit Irigarays Analyse, dass das Weibliche in der männlichen Ordnung als Mangel bzw. als Negation eingeschrieben sei. Wollen Frauen sich aus dieser Lage befreien müssen sie--bevor sie das Papier mit ihren Phantasien und Wünschen füllen können--zunächst ein leeres Blatt herstellen, d.h. die den Mangel verschleiernden Trugbilder wegwischen.

Das Schreiben dieses Mangels als Ermöglichung von Utopie steht im krassen Gegensatz zu den problematischen literarischen Entwürfen jüngster Zeit. Darin werden meist mit Bezugnahme auf matriarchale Verhältnisse Utopien weiblicher Unabhängigkeit als erreichtes Ziel ausgemalt. Das Personal dieser Utopien bilden Frauen, die autonome Wesen sind aufgrund der physischen Abwesenheit von Männern oder aber durch weibliche (Über)Macht. In diesen Entwürfen wird Frauen Macht verliehen und damit ein "Mangel" ausgeglichen, der nur innerhalb der Logik der männlichen Ordnung als solcher definiert ist.18 Mit einer "Ermangelung des Mangels" aber (Cixous) sind Frauen aus der symbolischen Ordnung ausgeschlossen, in die der einzelne Mann durch die symbolische Bedeutung der Kastrationsdrohung integriert wird, indem er über die Unterwerfung unter das Gesetz des Vaters gelangt. Macht- und Omnipotenzphantasien von Frauen bewegen sich innerhalb der Logik und Bedeutungen dieses Systems. Sie phantasieren, dass die Frau an die Stelle des Vaters tritt, indem der mit Macht versehene Mann vernichtet wird. Sie träumen den Traum des Sohnes zu Ende, den der Sohn sich abgewöhnen muss, um zu überleben und selbst Mann zu werden.

Der Mangel, von dem ich spreche, ist ein fundamental anderer: es ist der Mangel eines eigenen Begehrens, eines eigenen Bildes; er herrscht, solange die Frau in den Regeln der männlichen Ordnung denkt und schreibt. Das Wissen über den Mangel eines eigenen Begehrens herzustellen, erfordert und bedeutet, aus der männlichen Ordnung herauszutreten, sich dort herrschenden Definitionen von "Mangel" zu widersetzen, um eigene Wünsche erst freisetzen zu können. Nicht der Mangel von Macht, sondern der Mangel eigener Wünsche fesselt den Entwurf weiblicher Utopie.

Universität Hamburg

Anmerkungen

[1] Im Unterschied zu den USA, wo nicht alle, die sich mit "Frauenforschung" beschäftigen, von der Notwendigkeit eigener feministischer Methoden ausgehen.

[2] Silvia Bovenschen, Die imaginierte Weiblichkeit. Exemplarische Untersuchungen zu kulturgeschichtlichen und literarischen Präsentationsformen des Weiblichen. Frankfurt/M. 1979.

[3] Klaus Theweleit, Männerphantasien. 2 Bde. Frankfurt/M. 1977.

[4] Z.B. in den Publikationen von Gisela Dischner, Bettina von Arnim. Eine weibliche Sozialbiographie aus dem 19. Jahrhundert. Berlin 1977. Und: Caroline und der Jenaer Kreis. Berlin 1979. Aber auch in den Sammelbänden von Ursula Linnhoff: "Zur Freiheit, oh, zur einzig wahren"--Schreibende Frauen kämpfen um ihre Rechte. Köln 1979. Norgard Kohlhagen: Nicht nur dem Manne untertan. Frauen, die die Welt veränderten. Frankfurt/M. 1981. Auch in einigen Beiträgen in der

von H.-J. Schulz hg. Anthologie: Frauen. Porträts
aus zwei Jahrhunderten. Stuttgart 1981.

[5] Z.B. bei Renate Möhrmann, Die andere Frau. Eman-
zipationsansätze deutscher Schriftstellerinnen im Vor-
feld der Achtundvierziger-Revolution. Stuttgart 1977.
Und in der von Gisela Brinker-Gabler hg. Autobiograph-
ie von Fanny Lewald. Frankfurt/M. 1980.

[6] Sandra M. Gilbert/Susan Gubar, The Madwoman in
the Attic. The Woman Writer and the Nineteenth-Century
Literary Imagination. New Haven and London 1979.

[7] Claudia Honnegger/Bettina Heintz (Hg.), Die Listen der Ohnmacht. Zur Sozialgeschichte weiblicher
Widerstandsformen. Frankfurt/M. 1981.

[8] Um die Analyse von Frauen geschriebener Texte
anstelle theoretischer Postulate über "weibliches
Schreiben" geht es auch in dem von Irmela v.d. Lühe
hg. Band Entwürfe von Frauen in der Literatur des
20. Jahrhunderts. Berlin 1982.

[9] Vgl. etwa den von Brigitte Wartmann hg. Band
Weiblich-Männlich. Kulturgeschichtliche Spuren einer
verdrängten Weiblichkeit. Berlin 1980. Und: "Weibliche Produktivität." Ästhetik und Kommunication 47,
1982.

[10] So der nicht in allen Beiträgen eingelöste An-
spruch in dem von Ruth Grossmass und Christiane
Schmerl hg. Band Philosophische Beiträge zur Frauenforschung. Bochum 1981. In der von der Arbeitsstelle
"Sozial- Kultur- und Erziehungswissenschaftliche Frauenforschung" geplanten Tagung zum Thema "Mythos Frau"
im November 1982 in Berlin ist dies ausdrückliches
Tagungsziel. (Inzwischen ist die Tagung dokumentiert
in: Mythos Frau. Hg. v. Barbara Scheffer-Hegel/
Brigitte Wartmann. Berlin 1984.)

[11] Heide Göttner-Abendroth, Die Göttin und ihr
Heros. Die matriarchalen Religionen in Mythos, Mär-
chen und Dichtung. München 1981. Dies.: Die tanzende
Göttin. Prinzipien einer matriarchalen Ästhetik.
München 1982.

[12] Ich referiere hier knapp Ergebnisse, die ich an
anderer Stelle, am historischen Material entwickelt
und in einem grösseren Zusammenhang--Überlegungen für
eine feministische Literaturwissenschaft--ausgeführt

habe. Vgl. Sigrid Weigel, "Der schielende Blick.
Thesen zur Geschichte weiblicher Schreibpraxis," in:
Inge Stephan/Sigrid Weigel, Die verborgene Frau. Sechs
Beiträge zu einer feministischen Literaturwissen-
schaft. Berlin 1983.

[13] Elaine Showalter, A Literature of Their Own.
British Woman Novelists from Brontë to Lessing. Princeton 1977.

[14] Vgl. Marianne Schuller, "Literarische Szenerien
und ihre Schatten. Orte des Weiblichen in literarischen Produktionen." In: Ringvorlesung Frau und
Wissenschaft. Marburg, Sommersemester 1979. --Ähnlich
Gubar/Gilberts These von "women killing into art."

[15] Vgl. Luce Irigaray, Das Geschlecht das nicht eins
ist. Berlin 1979.

[16] Vgl. Helene Cixous, Die unendliche Zirkulation
des Begehrens. Berlin 1977. Und dies., Weiblichkeit
in der Schrift. Berlin 1980.

[17] Ingeborg Bachmann: "Literatur als Utopie."
(Frankfurter Vorlesungen. Probleme zeitgenössischer
Dichtung.) In: Werke. München 1978. Bd. 4., S. 258.

[18] Vgl. Sigrid Weigel, "Mit Siebenmeilenstiefeln
zur weiblichen Allmacht oder die kleinen Schritte aus
der männlichen Ordnung. Eine Kritik literarischer
Utopien von Frauen." In: Feministische Ringvorlesung.
Hg. v. Frauenreferat des ASTA. Universität Kiel.
Kiel 1984.

Jeannine Blackwell

Anonym, verschollen, trivial:
Methodological Hindrances in Researching
German Women's Literature

Frauenliteratur, like the terms Frauenroman and
Frauendichtung, is a two-way mirror. It is a distress-
ing reminder of the impotent and flowery sentimentality of Wilhelminian German literature: garden dwarfs,
the Gartenlaube, tüchtige Hausfrauen, Hedwig Courths-
Mahler, and Vicki Baum. It is harmless literature, to
be classified next to the children's stories, the cookbooks, and home improvements. Yet with this term Frauenliteratur, as with so many, there is a cutting edge.
Is Frauenliteratur really what Treitschke and Goedeke
tell us it is? Is it not also the letters Caroline and
Dorothea wrote, Bettina's Armenbuch, Gabriele Reuter's
social protest? Were not these also by, for, and
about women in Germany? To discover what Frauenliteratur was and is, scholars today must look through that
dark, distorting mirror of literary history. Anticipating and identifying the cracks in that history, feminist critics must reshape the critical tools to deal
with the anonymous, the unrecognized, the uncanonized,
the "trivial"; to reconstruct or rediscover the verschollen; and to locate and describe the dear ladies
who read the books back then.

The other side of the cracked mirror of literary
history is Frauenliteratur today. It is the product of
contemporary critical female authors for a predominantly female audience; it is also the reestablished or
discovered tradition of women authors such as Sidonie
Zäunemann (1714-1740), Therese Huber (1764-1829), and
Gertrud Kolmar (1894-1943?). Often a literature of the
"other Germany" -- critical, republican, socialist,
utopian, or feminist -- it is not harmless, impotent
droolings. This excavation work brings out the straight-
forward, graphic, even aggressive side of German women's literary culture. This research has grown out of
the second women's movement in both Europe and the
United States. Its new female mentality, new consciousness of history and the private sphere demand a fresh
reading of the old texts. In this reading, feminists
cannot rely trustingly on that cracked mirror of German literary history. We must reread everything and
question the verity of every fact already given.

The great reference works of the nineteenth century are some of the most important tools we have to reconstruct that literature. Knowing the history of these works will give feminist scholars today an idea of how Frauenliteratur was defined, which pieces were included, and which were omitted. A brief examination of the process of literary analysis in Germany will underscore the pitfalls of such reference works. These massive undertakings must be checked for factual error, but more importantly, they must be seen in conjunction with and contrast to the movements of social and political change within the German area.

The establishment of modern German universities, under the leadership of the brothers Grimm and Humboldt, brought in a model of scholarly research which became paradigmatic for Germanistik as well as for the natural sciences. The linguistisch-literaturwissenschaftliche method of philological research, historical dating, biographical data, study of origins and development started by the collections of Herder and the brothers Grimm put literature first into its historical context, and then into national and linguistic groupings; its authorial origins were sought out if possible. Criticism was no longer merely aesthetic, moral, and philosophical, but rather historical. With this group of scholars and with the establishment of new universities at Berlin, Göttingen, and elsewhere, the separation of the writing scholar and the artistic scholar was completed. While it had been customary up to the eighteenth century for the two fields to be combined -- one thinks here of Opitz, later Lessing, Herder, and Wieland, who wrote both scholarly treatises and creative works -- this era brings about the division and professionalization of poet and scholar.

The division of labor between the Gelehrten and the Dichter that prevailed after the late 18th century was a boon to women authors. Since they had been and continued to be excluded from university study (with a few loudly proclaimed exceptions) and had little opportunity to learn the classics or consistent orthography, they had been essentially shut out from literary production. The new division of literary labor, combined with the spiritual justification of women's literary forms in Pietist confessional literature, changed that situation abruptly. With

the change came a rise in the number of women novelists, after them the female leaders of the Romantic
salons, and later the prolific women authors of the
1830s and 1840s. Feminist scholars have successfully
reconstructed the contours of this women's literature,
based on the rather haphazardly gathered lists
of names we have left. Ironically, these names seem
frequently to be ones attached to the great men of
the time by blood, passion, or marriage: Sophie von
LaRoche, Caroline de la Motte-Fouque, Bettina von
Arnim, Caroline and Dorothea Schlegel, and Johanna
Schopenhauer. Nevertheless, we do have a continuous
corpus of works with authors that bears the name of
Frauenliteratur from this period. The success of
these authors in an anonymous book market and the
popularity of their literary Frauenideal contributed
to this continuity.

Yet this same division of literary labor asserted
a caste of university educated arbiters of taste who
then criticized and categorized literature professionally. As necessary as this academic work was and
is, considering the volume of creative literature
since 1800, it nevertheless limited the defining of
worthwhile literature to the analytical powers of a
few. These few had no women among them, of course,
until one of the first literary critics and scholars,
Ricarda Huch, joined academe in the 20th century.[1]
While this does not mean that women's literature could
not be treated equally in literary criticism, it did
mean that the standards of Literaturwissenschaft re-
tained the cast of the hierarchical, exclusive, authoritarian German university system, as it developed
in the later nineteenth century. Carrying the methods
of Herder and Grimm to artistic and fictional literature, these scholars were concerned with the great
names, trends, and periods which could be organized,
as in the natural sciences, according to genus, development, and heredity. It is to this group that we
owe the widespread use of terms such as Novelle,
Bildungsroman, Klassik, Sturm und Drang, and many
more. Their search for categorization led them, however, into inordinate emphasis on the long term
consistent "growth" of the individual author and his
(sic) work, and into exclusionary tactics when dealing with literature which did not fit the generic
or authorial model.

The professional search for authorial validity
expanded with the generation after Hegel and the

positivistic research in the Historical School of
Leopold von Ranke. This period and approach has given
Germanistik some of its most essential tools: the
Allgemeine Deutsche Biographie, Goedeke's Grundriss,
Treitschke's history, and many other literary histories. At the same time that feminists must recognize and value these herculean efforts at detail
and biographical research, they must also acknowledge the pitfalls of such an authorial and historical
approach: those works which fall out of the frame --
the anonymous, the unreviewed, the literature which
is not of the classical, historical, or political
world, which is not of a particular School or group --
are not treated as frequently, not given as much
space, not weighted as heavily. Authors whose oeuvre
is small, perhaps only one or two novels or slim
volumes, are simply dismissed. In an age in which
name and family were still ascendant, those whose
names were not fixed were often lost in the index.
One has only to look for "Therese geb. Heyne gesch.
Forster verh. Huber" to see the problems in naming
the names of great women.

While the more charitable of these cataloguers
of the later 19th century did include the major women
authors in their works, the patriarchal attitudes of
the period meant that their connections with great
men weighed more heavily than their original works or
their connections with other women authors. The more
aggressively misogynist or exclusivist historians, who
were aware of the beginning women's movement initiated by Louise Otto-Peters in the 1860s and growing stead-
ily until World War I, agreed with social Darwinists
Arthur Schopenhauer, Friedrich Nietzsche, and Stefan
George about the negative role women had to play in
literature and public life. A copious body of anti-
feminist tracts and responses based on "scientific"
findings also emerges in this era.[2] Thus the highpoint in positivistic literary research was also the
highpoint in the first German women's movement and the
highpoint in antifeminist writings in philosophy
and the natural sciences -- the recognized "higher"
disciplines which Literaturwissenschaft took as models. Finally, the post-1848 period marked the apo-
theosis of the German housewife and mother in the
family journals and in popular culture: this was the
time of the increasing stress on cleanliness and
women's diligence in the home, of a thoroughly do-
mesticated wife even among the petite bourgeoisie and

working class, as the majority of Germans became ur-
banized and literate in the last quarter of the nineteenth century. Housewifery acquired a frantic patriotism as an institution in this era.

As the strength of Social Darwinism, the Kultur-
kampf, and the Socialist prohibition waned toward the
turn of the century, so did the prodigious efforts of
the positivist literary "scientists". The 1890s
brought a new aestheticism to avant garde literary en-
deavors, led by the exclusively male George circle.
This new direction was enhanced by the werkimmanente
criticism of Dilthey, Gundolf and their followers to
the detriment of other literary trends. This avant
garde appears at the same time that bourgeois and pa-
trician women authors such as Gabriele Reuter, Helene
Böhlau, and Maria Janitschek, and Clara Viebig begin
their "nervöse Kunst"[3] -- a socially critical, neu-
rotic, urbane, sexually graphic and even brutal art.
Simultaneously, a conscious literature by and for the
working class is initiated by Adelheid Popp's autobiography in 1895. Of this "other Germany" of the
powerless we find precious little in the reference
works, and it filters out totally in modern compendia
such as Frenzels's Daten deutscher Dichtung, the Auf-
bau Verlag's Erläuterungen zur deutschen Literatur,
or the 1982 Metzler Deutsche Literatur-Geschichte.

This new art, reflecting socialism and Freudian-
ism, finds no outlet in the subsequent periodization
of the era: not Naturalist drama or Neoromantic or
Symbolist verse, it falls between the pidgeonholes.
Its themes and form are only recognized as a literary
category when Robert Musil, Alfred Döblin and Bertolt
Brecht give them authority and authenticity.

One source of this filtering process in today's
reference works are the almost irreplaceable omissions
during the Third Reich. Not only did National Socialist policy dictate the prohibition or exile of most
of the best women authors -- Claire Goll, Else Lasker-
Schüler, and Anna Seghers are examples -- it also
brought into disrepute those liberal humanist scholars like Heinrich Spiero who had actually dealt at
length with women's writings. By cutting off scholars
who addressed socially critical and feminist creative
literature, Nazi ideology both stopped immediate research and publications in those fields, and also end-
ed the methodological tradition: there was no one to
pass it on to the next generation of scholars.

While Marxist scholarship did recover in exile and in
a displaced tradition abroad with a new generation of
male scholars, such a scholarly interest group was
not available for women's literature. Here Hannah
Arendt, Ingeborg Drewitz, and Luise Rinser (less a
scholar than the former) stand alone in a tradition
of female authors who were also essayists and moral/
intellectual leaders. Moreover, Frauenliteratur was
particularly bound to its audience. The one concrete
justification given for scholarly interest in it --
its popularity among women readers and bestseller
status -- was abruptly undermined in the Third Reich
years. When all socially critical women authors were
prohibited, they were cut off from their only reading
public. The hiatus in humanistic and socially critical
theory affected Frauenliteratur even more than bourgeois aesthetic literature: while the latter could
be partially restored by continuity in criticism
abroad, Frauenliteratur, as a creative process and
as a critical field, essentially ceased to exist.

After the war, critical theory rebuilt on the
ruins of the German university. As in so many other
cultural areas, the Germanies assumed the prevailing
literary critical methods of their respective occu-
pation powers. In the West, this meant New Criticism
until well into the 1960s. The West dictated authorial behavior as well: a generation of angry young men
in the style of Norman Mailer or Holden Caulfield --
Böll, Grass, Weiss, Frisch, Handke -- dominated the
West German literary scene for three decades. Here,
again, there was little room for a critical Frauenliteratur.

Social upheaval beginning in the 1960s revived
a new self-awareness in socially critical young
people and led them to theory, praxis, and literature.
The methodological revisions of the New Social Historians which grew out of the university movement in
Western Europe unearthed a forgotten tradition of
German protest and documentary literature and reestablished the connection between history and everyday domestic and working life. This new historicity,
combined with a native and USA-imported wave of feminism, spurred on the investigation of a lost women's
literary tradition in the West. It also gave birth to
a new and critical generation of women authors, women's presses and bookshops, and feminist critics in
the Federal Republic of Germany as well as in the
United States.[4]

44

The German Democratic Republic critical tradition, on the other hand, followed Marxist literary analysis, and was therefore keyed to realism, daily life and oppression under capitalism from its beginnings. A certain naiveté in facing women's special and continuing inequality, however, rendered early women characters stiff and artificial. With time, a group of women scholars also developed in the East, as they gained access to academic and lectoral positions. Popular uprisings in the fifties and sixties in Eastern Europe contributed to an impatience and disillusionment with the status quo of socialism in the East and led directly to the generation of young critical authors, many of whom were women, many of whom also turned to the documentary and the novel of development. Others prepared the groundwork for the New Subjectivity. Scholars such as Annemarie Auer, Sigrid Damm, and Edith Anderson, authors such as Christa Wolf, Maxie Wander, Sarah Kirsch, and Irmtraud Morgner exemplify these trends.

Keeping in mind the growth of critical reception and production of socially aware Frauenliteratur, feminist critics can locate the peculiar danger areas of the scholarly literature on it since 1770. Knowing the problems, we can develop strategies for making most productive use of the research tools. I have listed here some suggestions for the wary feminist scholar.

1. Authority and authenticity.

The very word Autor connotes creative power. In Western thought it is frequently associated with the masculine generative act, as Susan Gubar has pointed out. God, in this philosophy, is the author of the universe. By usurping the term "author" for women, female writers and critics are contradicting a hierarchy that runs, roughly, God -- Martin Luther -- Goethe -- Mann -- "everyone else" -- women authors. Dichter likewise has a traditional reception as a professional, idealized genius of which Goethe is the paradigm and measure. Feminist critics should be aware of the implicit comparisons in these terms, and ask themselves if this type of authenticity (that is, one ordained by a spiritual, intellectual, or aesthetic hierarchy) is the type which gives credence to women's writing. I think that women's writing derives its authenticity from this source in some, but not most, cases. Here feminist critics would be wise to

45

question both intent and effect of women's writing to see just where its authority begins. Is it grounded in an uncluttered depiction of the real world? Is it a special vision based biologically? Is it a certain religious or mystical gift? Is it the all too clear view of the oppressed from down below? It is to misunderstand the authority of women's writings to push them into the framework of almost exclusively male movements which happen to be simultaneous (Enlightenment, Storm and Stress, Romanticism, Expressionism) and then find them wanting.

2. Periodization.

Let us glance at the categories of the German canon -- Baroque, Enlightenment, Storm and Stress, Romanticism, Classicism, Poetic Realism, Naturalism, and Expressionism. Critical recognition of these movements is directly proportional to the elite humanistic university education and the class standing of their authors. We have only to look at the literary movements which are not as well represented in the canon -- Sentimentality, Junges Deutschland, "Nervöse Kunst," Proletkult -- to see that male, university educated, conservative scholars feel an affinity for art produced by their own sexual, educational, and political peer group. This is understandable, even acceptable, if they acknowledge their bias. An extreme example of this, without a critical evaluation of bias, is the inordinate emphasis of traditional literary criticism, as carried out in graduate reading lists, anthologies, and literary histories, on the small George circle, as well as on Poetic Realism.

Feminist critics should question the validity of these categories for groups whose lives and literature did not come from such an educational or class background. I would simply point out here an example, the period from 1790 to 1830, commonly designated as Classicism and Romanticism. At a time of unique and prolific novel publication and salon activity, women's literary lives fit into neither frame. Women did not write Romantic novels or poetry -- they wrote Gesellschaftsromane, Erziehungsromane, described Frauenideale, and organized literary intercourse in the semi-public domestic sphere of the salon. If I had to give a name to their literary culture, I would call it Salonism -- the mediation of literature and social exchange by women be-

46

tween domestic and public life. Women, with a different literary tradition and different cultural role
expectations, were simply marching to a different
drummer.

At the same time, it is crucial to understand
that many women authors did indeed adhere to the predominant movements of their time, and often combined
the feminine and masculine literary traditions in
fresh ways. Bettina von Arnim's works, for example,
integrate the female epistolary form and women's
romance with the hegemonic literary content of her
day. While feminist critics should be the first
to acknowledge these creative syntheses, it should
not be to the detriment of unrecognized literary
trends.

3. The Great Artist.

A conceit of Western literary analysis has been
the creative life of the Great Man of Letters. His
youth is lavish and his education thorough, but he
is misunderstood by mundane and authoritarian family
and forced into a respectable and class-appropriate
profession. He revolts early, produces precocious,
effervescent, highly autobiographical works, mellows
as he assumes responsibilities in his community, and
refines his style in his midlife masterworks, which
are generic jewels. Finally in old age, a national
literary institution, he turns to the Great Ideas of
Mankind in his last works, and often he leaves a
journal of his significant life. Women in his life
are love inspiration, sources for naive stories and
pre-literary forms, and support systems of mother,
wife, sister, and patient devotee.

The myth of the literary woman which I set
against this conceit is substantially different. A
bourgeois household teaches her the feminine arts
of painting, reading and writing in French, religion,
sewing, and housekeeping, while a male relative in-
sists on giving her some sort of scientific or Classical learning. She reads some forbidden books. She is
married early to a man much older and worldwise than
she, who teaches her to be a sophisticate's wife and
who travels with her through Europe. She has too many
children too fast, and tragedy sets in -- suicide,
death of husband or children, or divorce -- and she
must save the family from financial ruin, war, or
dangerous politics. She hurriedly produces trans-

lations, travelogues, cookbooks, children's stories, articles, reviews, and a few long creative works. She hides most of this production in anonymity or under the name of her husband. She remarries or has more children, and later in life she writes more creative literature. She gives advice and support to younger women authors. She is mourned only by her loyal female readership. She is Sophie von LaRouche, Therese Huber, Johanna Schopenhauer or Bettina von Arnim.

When we try to force her lifework into the pattern of his, several tattered bits are lost; the variety in her production and reproduction of the literary culture in the "non-creative" genres; the rhythm of her spurts of writing rather than a continuous, organic growth; and her sense of responsibility to the next generation of women's literature.

More frequently than even this attempt to measure her literary life against his, we find that she is simply not given her own billing: she is merely a subplot in the myth of the Great Man's life. I will give two examples of how this operated in Meusel's Das gelehrte Teutschland (1796-1834) and in the Allgemeine Deutsche Biographie.

Therese Huber (1764-1829), although a prolific author and editor of Cotta's Morgenblatt für die gebildeten Stände, remained anonymous by choice during her marriages to Georg Forster and Ludwig Ferdinand Huber. Das gelehrte Teutschland offers important contemporary information on her, but it is organized in a way that reflects her role merely in the lives of her men. Therese appears in all three alphabetical series by Meusel and his later editors. The first citation, in 1802[5], notes that many of Therese's works were published under the name of Ludwig Ferdinand, but this information is found under his biographical entry, since she has none. This disclaimer does not say which works are his and hers and is located at the very end of the entry. "Viele Uebersetzungen und Aufsätze, die ihm zugeschrieben werden, sind von seiner Frau, einer Tochter des geheimen Justitzraths Heyne zu Göttingen und Georg Forsters abgeschiedenen Weibes." Note that she is defined as wife, but crosslisted as daughter and ex-wife. Meusel does not question his data, in the same entry, about L.F. Huber's contributions to Flora Teutschlands Tochter geweiht or Taschenkalender für Damen.

By the 1821 Meusel series, Therese was the anonymous editor of the influential Morgenblatt, and as

such deserved her own alphabetical listing.[6] The suspicions raised about the origins of L.F Huber's
works in 1802 is ignored, however. In his entry,
Ludwig is credited with more stories and the publication of the last part of his collected works in
1810. He died in 1804. Therese is given credit for
some of her books and noted as "Mitherausgeberin des
Morgenblatts"; the works attributed to her husband
are brushed aside in a final comment: "Ihrer geschah
bereits Erwähnung im 9.B.(uch)unter der Notiz von
ihrem Manne: Huber (L.F.)."

By 1831, after Therese's death, the final Meusel
series[7] had compiled all the information on her life
and work. Here we find that all narrative works
which were published under her husband's name from
1795 to 1804 (their whole married life) belong to
her; and that she edited the Morgenblatt since 1817
(actually 1816). Germanists are fortunate that Meusel's editors were able to trace and acknowledge
her works, even if it took 30 years and three versions. One can see, however, that the tendency is to
classify women under the heading of their significant
males unless there are unavoidable indications of her
independent work. As Dorothea Schlegel's novel
Florinde is still today bound with Friedrich Schlegel's
collected works in some libraries, feminists must
remember that women authors often do not have a
name of their own.

A variation on the curriculum vitae of the Great
Artist is the judgement of a woman author, not by
her literary merits, but rather by how she performed
in her subplot of the male life. She is evaluated on
her success as a wife and mother, rather than on her
writing. Here we have a classic case of a generation
of women authors being read through the lives of
their sons: Johanna Schopenhauer (1770-1838). Johanna,
a popular Weimar author in the 1820s and 30s, has
suffered a bad press ever since she broke off relations with her son Arthur after 1811. When the impoverished widow took in a minor poet as a boarder
in Weimar and developed an intimate relationship
with him, Arthur objected to the freedom of his mother's living arrangements. After much argument, she
disowned him, writing him out of her meager will.
Hugo Liepmann in the Allgemeine deutsche Biographie
entry on Arthur laments the bad feeling between
Arthur and "seiner Mutter, einer reichbegabten, aber

kalten, gegen den Sohn lieblosen Frau."[8] Friedrich
Kummer relates in the accompanying article on Johanna
that Arthur distanced himself from "der weit ober-
flächlicheren Mutter, die ihn niemals als den über-
legenen Genius anzuerkennen vermochte."[9] One won-
ders what purpose all this unnatural emphasis on
motherhood serves. Feminists should thus learn to
consider denigrating commentary on women as material
extraneous to a real literary analysis.

4. Gender and Genre

The hierarchy of literary types is yet another
outgrowth of elite humanistic education and scholarly hierarchy. Following the model of Classics and
the sciences, scholarly critics ranked literature
according to worth. The plethora of modern genres
have been graded informally as well: by difficulty
of technique, obtuseness, philosophical content,
experiment with form, or erudition. While generic
categories up to the nineteenth century were based
on the Classics, the high genres were limited to
authors with an education in the classics. Knowledge of complicated meter, French and Italian art,
drama, and poetry, were prerequisites to mastery
of the hegemonic forms. Women who had no access
to that education either "failed" in those genres
(Anna Louise Karsch) or turned to other forms.
The genres women often chose, by their very association with the uneducated readers, were devalued.
Specific examples here are the sentimental novel,
tableaux vivantes (unless done by Goethe), Frau-
enromane, the post-1850 family journals and serial
novels, and "nervöse Kunst."

A firm refusal of the hierarchy of genre is
a basic premise for feminist scholarship. While
erudition and stylistic finesse certainly have
their place in literary judgements, categorical rejection of forms will not only endanger experimental
genre, it also ignores the specific virtuoso contributions, of individual women authors who worked out
of no tradition. The equation of Frauenliteratur and
Trivialliteratur is an outgrowth of this hierarchy
of forms. The vague outlines and prejudicial character of this designation makes it a useless de-
scriptor for feminist critics. It is, however, of
great significance in women's literary history and
thus deserves critical investigation in the recep-

tion history of women's literature. The equation of the two, which is more or less an assumption in the trailblazing first analyses of Trivialliteratur in the 1960s[10], must be investigated from both sides: What constitutes women's culture and what is triviality? By whose definition? Which male authored and female authored literature is included, which excluded? What effect does this genre assignment have on the reading public, on critical reception, on canonization (through library purchase, classroom use, anthologies, and literary histories)? Until these questions are asked and answered, feminist scholars must be careful to use the least judgement-laden terms they can find. They must find plausible explanations for why women generally make use of certain genres (fictional prose, nature poetry, documentary) and not others (drama, rhetorical essays): this, too, is womens' literary history.

5. Reading backwards in the mirror.

Until feminist Germanistics develops its new tools for reference, we will need to use the traditional works. In order to exploit them effectively, we have to learn to read them wrong side out, against the grain, and with a reversed hierarchy of ideas.

We have to read articles and entries from end to beginning, to correct for the misplaced emphasis in women's lives, to find the hidden anomalies, the tragedies, the irritants in their works. An example of this is the Allgemeine deutsche Biographie entry on Friederike Helene Unger (1751-1813)[11], an impenetrable two-page-long paragraph in Fraktur. It tells readers first that her articles on history and economics are too wordy, but interesting; it praises her for being a housewife and helping her publisher husband; it lauds her for writing a cookbook, a patriotic soldiers' reader, a critique of a hymnal, a children's book; it describes her translations of Beaumarchais, Marivaux, Mercier, Molière, and Rousseau into German. Her novels are then discussed, and in the final quarter of the article we arrive at "ihr bekanntestes und wichtigstes Buch," Julchen Grünthal. It is damned with faint praise. Thus this very popular and important novel, with the unmentioned first lesbian scene in German literature, is buried toward the end. The article closes with what is called

her major achievement: she introduced Goethe to
Zelter, the song writer. In order to discover Unger's
contribution to German women's literature, we have
to seek out the buried information, distrust a negative review, and even reject an inaccurate plot
summary.

Reading backwards means investigating all later
editions personally and not believing attributions,
alleged translations, and the dating given by reference works. Feminists must read all revised editions of bibliographies, biographies, necrologues,
Nachträge, and afterwords -- with a critical eye
for gaps and contradictions. We must be suspicious
of mistakes repeated and sanctified by repetition in
scholarship. The unauthorized sequel to Julchen
Grünthal, rejected by Unger herself in a preface, was
confused with her own sequel (in which Julchen's
lesbian scene occurs). Goedeke and Meusel misunderstand the data and assume that Unger authorized
J.G. Stutz's continuation.[12] Michael Hadley, in
Romanverzeichnis. Bibliographie der zwischen 1750-
1800 erschienenen Erstausgaben (Bern: Peter Lang,
1977), does not detect the real second volume by
Unger which appeared in 1798, but lists Stutz's.

Title pages, prefaces, and pictures also give
feminists information that has been overlooked. Here
one can find a preface to a first person female
Robinsonade of 1766 signed by "Jacobine W.", but
attributed to Christian Gottlob Hauffe. While it is
possible that he did write this as a fiction himself,
internal evidence points to the contrary, and I have
found no evidence to show that there was not actually
a woman in Regensburg who authored the work; yet
the library at Regensburg, and Robinsonade experts
P.B. Gove and Jürgen Fohrmann,[13] using handed-down
bibliographies, continue to use the Hauffe attri-
bution without question. Thus the questionable data
is given reinforcing confirmation by competent
authorities.

The hidden plot, the class and sexual relationships of characters, can often be read from the
etchings commonly used to illustrate early women's
literature. The ostensible purpose and philosophy
of writing is often incorporated into the preface,
along with autobiographical details and educational
background; title pages will frequently mention "von

der Verfasserin von...", and thus give information
on a continuing literary production.

The special works on women's literature, which
began appearing already in 1715[14] and crested in the
1890s[15], can give feminist scholars more information
on authors. They must be read critically, because
the prevailing ideologies of patriotism, antifemin-
ism, domestic science, or religious morality often
color their listing and lead to extraordinary exclu-
sions, such as that of Louise Aston or Johanna
Kinkel. Women's newspapers, from the journals established by Sophie von LaRoche up to the most recent feminist monthlies, review women's literature,
treat Frauenliteratur with much more consistency
than the regular critical review works, and are
often not catalogued or indexed in major literary
compendia. They, too, must often be read backwards
to find what women were actually doing, why they
really read the books; all too frequently they are
defending themselves against charges of atheism,
republicanism, immorality, and unfeminity, and go
to extremes to prove otherwise: they sneak past
Fanny Lewald's long affair with Adolph Stahr and
Gabriele Reuter's child out of wedlock. Nevertheless
they are fruitful sources of names, titles, and family and literary connections.

Keeping this skill of backwards reading intact,
feminists must also build up a body of their own reference works. Some important work has already been
done: Elke Frederiksen is currently editing the bio-
bibliography of German women authors in print for
the Modern Language Association's edition of non-
English Women in Print. Elisabeth Friedrich's massive lexicon of women authors[16] is a useful tool
for locating biographical facts on specific writers,
even though it does not provide bibliographic information on their primary works. Gisela Brinker-
Gabler's anthology of German women poets since 1500[17]
is an auspicious beginning for research in that
genre, as is Elke Fredriksen's anthology of the
Frauenfrage in Deutschland 1865-1915.[18] A critical
anthology of women's journals in Germany edited by
Ruth-Esther Geiger and Sigrid Weigel[19] gives necessary
titles and excerpts from significant essays and reviews.

Starting with these critical feminist landmark
works, we have a base now to build on. Now we must
move beyond two critical problems of non-American

feminist literature to create the rest of our tools.
The first dilemma is related to lack of research
in the politics, history and science affecting women's lives. There has been an unavoidable dependence on American and French research, while the
specific historical conditions of women in Germany,
Austria, and Switzerland remained undiscovered.
We applied theory and praxis on to the German language area without knowing if the same or similar
conditions held. I think particularly here of the
lack of feminist research in the Reformation, the
Thirty Years War and witch persecution, and the
Third Reich exile. This absence of historical data
means that our research has tended toward general-
ities based solely on Marxist abstractions undiffer-
entiated   for women and thus toward ahistoricity.
Of course, feminist scholarship cannot exist without a healthy dose of critical historicizing. As
the work of historians like Annemarie Truger continues, these dark holes in German women's history
should disappear. Meanwhile, we will have to reconstruct female literacy rates, family policy,
legal status, and community organizing as best
we can. This means digging, reading legal codes,
and working with statistics.

The second problem confronting feminist method-
ology in the interim is the dilemma of the "special feminist issue." If our reference works are
to benefit all scholars, they must be read and
used beyond our specialty. It is vital to have in-
house journals, but we must see to it that anthologies and reference tools are purchased by libraries and put on reading lists. We should take care
to have more feminist papers appearing in general
Germanistics journals and more talks in non-femin-
ist general sections of conferences. The participation of Women in German members at the Tri-
Centennial conferences is just one example of finding our own public. We must remember that the un-
charitable misogynists/purists in our field want
us precisely there, on the sidelines, talking to
ourselves. Let us deny them that pleasure.

Balancing carefully between ahistoricity and
feminist pidgeonholing, we turn to the new tasks:
what we need. First we need a thorough bibliography
of primary works -- a new Lexicon deutscher Frauen

der Feder, with lists of reviews, first editions, and short synopses. We lack a study on the collaboration of women authors such as Caroline de la Motte-Fouque/Amalie von Helwig, Bettina and Gisela von Arnim, Caroline and Dorothea Schlegel, Sophie von LaRoche and the authors she published, and Klara Zetkin/Rosa Luxemburg. There is no study of the economics of women's publication in Germany: income, self-support, popularity, and authorship. We should investigate the influences current in certain cities, salons, and families among women: Berlin, Vienna, Frankfurt, Hamburg; the families of LaRoche/Brentano, Charlotte Birch-Pfeiffer, and her daughter Wilhelmine von Hillern, Anna Louise Karsch and her granddaughter Helmine von Chezy, and Philippine Gatterer Engelhard and her great-granddaughter Gabriele Reuter. Finally, we need to write a history of German women's literature -- to reweigh the trivial, to restore the verschollen, and to name the anonymous.

Michigan State University

Notes

[1] While the höhere Mädchenschulen doubled in number from 1860 to 1901 (from 47 to 110), women had no Lyzeen which prepared them for entrance into German universities until 1893; they were generally admitted to academic study (without admission to the Staatsexamen) after 1897/1898.

[2] The most influential of these anti-feminist writings were: Paul Julius Möbius, Über den physiologischen Schwachsinn des Weibes (Halle: Marhold, 1900), Jakob Schapiro, Ihr sollt nicht gleich sein. Eine biologische Betrachtung über zwei bedeutsame Zeitströmungen (Zürich: Caesar Schmidt, 1904), Otto Weininger, Geschlecht und Charakter (Vienna and Leipzig: Braumüller, 1903). The most telling response to these misogynist critics was Hedwig Dohm, Die Anti-Feministen. Ein Buch der Verteidigung (Berlin: F. Dümmler, 1902).

[3] Heinrich Spiero, Geschichte der deutschen Frauendichtung seit 1800 (Leipzig: B.G. Teubner, 1913) pp. 88f.

[4] Works of the New Social Historians include:
Ingeborg Weber-Kellermann, Die deutsche Familie.
Versuch einer Sozialgeschichte (Frankfurt: Suhrkamp,
1974) and Sozialgeschichte der Familie in der Neuzeit
Europas. Neue Forschungen, edited by Werner Conze
(Stuttgart: Ernst Klett, 1976).
     Historical works specifically on the women's
movement which grew out of the New Social History:
     Werner Thönessen, Frauenemanzipation. Politik
und Literatur der deutschen Sozialdemokratie zur
Frauenbewegung 1863-1933 (Frankfurt: Europäische
Verlagsanstalt, 1969)
     Margrit Twellmann, Die deutsche Frauenbewegung.
Ihre Anfänge und erste Entwicklung 1843-1889, 2 vols.
(Meisenheim am Glan: Anton Hain, 1972, second volume
Kronberg: Athenäum, 1976)
     Richard J. Evans, The Feminist Movement in
Germany 1894-1933 (London: SAGE Publications, 1976)
     Jean Quataert, Reluctant Feminists in German
Social Democracy 1885-1917 (Princeton: Princeton
University Press, 1979).

     The following are special issues of journals
which deal primarily with women's literature or history:
     Aesthetik und Kommunikation 7 (September 1976),
which contains the programmatic feminist essay by
Silvia Bovenschen, "Über die Frage: gibt es eine
weibliche Aesthetik?", 60-75.
     Kursbuch 47 (March 1977), which includes Bar-
bara Duden's historical essay, "Das schöne Eigentum,
Zur Herausbildung des bürgerlichen Frauenbildes an
der Wende vom 18. zum 19. Jahrhundert," 125-142.
     New German Critique 13 (Winter, 1978) Special
feminist issue on contemporary German culture.
     Wolfenbüttler Studien zur Aufklärung 3 (1976),
edited by Günter Schulz (Bremen: Jacobi, 1976) contains several articles on women's literary forms and
education in the eighteenth century.

[5] Georg Christoph Hamberger and Johann Georg
Meusel, Das gelehrte Teutschland oder Lexikon der
jetzt lebenden Schriftsteller 1796-1834 (reprint
Hildesheim: Georg Olms, 1966), vol. 9, p. 630.

[6] Hamberger and Meusel, vol. 18, p. 223.

[7] Hamberger and Meusel, vol. 22(2), pp. 858-860.

[8] *Allgemeine deutsche Biographie* (Leipzig: Dunck-er and Humbolt, 1875-1912) 32: 335.

[9] *Allgemeine deutsche Biographie* 32: 346-349.

[10] Impetus for these studies of trivial litera-ture grew out of the sociological approach of Jürgen Habermas, *Strukturwandel der Öffentlichkeit* (Neuwied and Berlin: Luchterhand, 1962). They are: Martin Greiner, *Die Entstehung der modernen Unterhaltungs-literatur. Studien zum Trivialroman des achtzehnten Jahrhunderts* (Reinbek bei Hamburg: Rowohlt, 1964) and Marion Beaujean, *Der Trivialroman in der zweiten Hälfte des 18. Jahrhunderts. Die Ursprünge des moder-nen Unterhaltungsromans* (Bonn: Bouvier, 2nd ed., 1969). Studies written in a more informal style are Gustav Sichelschmidt, *Liebe, Mord und Abenteuer. Eine Ge-schichte der deutschen Unterhaltungsliteratur* (Berlin: Haude and Spener, 1969) and Gabriele Strecker, *Frauen-träume, Frauentränen. Über den deutschen Frauenroman* (Weilheim/Oberbayern: Otto Wilhelm Barth, 1969).

[11] *Allgemeine deutsche Biographie* 93: 293-296.

[12] Johann Georg Meusel, *Lexikon der vom Jahr 1750 bis 1800 verstorbenen teutschen Schriftsteller*, orig-inal edition 1802-1806 (reprint Hildesheim: G. Olms, 1967-68) 9:170ff and Karl Goedeke, *Grundriss zur Ge-schichte der deutschen Dichtung aus den Quellen*, 2nd edition (Dresden: L. Ehlermann, 1884-1966) V,221.

[13] The text in question is: *Merkwürdige und aus-serordentliche Begebenheiten einer kosakischen Stand-esperson, von ihr selbst zu ihrem und anderer Vergnü-gen beschrieben* (Regensburg: Joh. Leopold Montag, 1766), which is attributed to Hauffe in the listings of P.B. Gove, *The Imaginary Voyage in Prose Fiction. A History of its Criticism and a Guide for its Study with an Annotated Checklist of 215 Imaginary Voyages from 1700 to 1800* (London: Holland Press, 1941, 2nd edition 1961) and Jürgen Fohrmann, *Abenteuer und Bürgertum. Zur Geschichte der deutschen Robinsonade im 18. Jahrhundert* (Stuttgart: J.B. Metzler, 1981).

[14] Georg Christian Lehms, *Teutschlands Galante Poetinnen mit sinnreichen und netten Proben* (Frank-furt: Samuel Tobias Hocker, 1715).

[15] The following are the most significant of histories of German women's literature:

Ludwig Geiger, Dichter und Frauen. Vorträge und Abhandlungen (Berlin: Gebrüder Paetel, 1896) has essays on the women around Goethe, Schiller, and the Romantics, and the love relationships of several poets; he discusses the female characters in Otto Ludwig and Guy de Maupassant; the only woman author whose works and life he treats in detail is Fanny Lewald.

Heinrich Gross, Deutschlands Dichterinen (sic) und Schriftstellerinen (sic). Eine literar-historische Skizze, second revised edition (Vienna: Carl Gerold's Sohn, 1882) is the richest in data on and connections between women authors. The first edition was a private printing of an outline of the work.

Louise Otto-Peters, leader of the early German women's movement and herself an author, produced several biographical collections of women's lives as an expansion of German history: Merkwürdige und geheimnisvolle Frauen (Leipzig: H. Matthes, 1868) presents stories of women accused of witchcraft; Einflussreiche Frauen aus dem Volke (Leipzig: H. Matthes, 1869) stresses the political and religious contribution of middle and lower class women throughout history; and Frauenleben im deutschen Reich (Leipzig: M. Schäfer, 1876) reviews the lives of predominantly aristocratic women from the Enlightenment and earlier.

Sophie Pataky, Lexikon deutscher Frauen der Feder. Eine Zusammenstellung der seit 1840 erschienenen Werke weiblicher Autoren nebst Biographieen (sic) der lebenden und einem Verzeichnis der Pseudonyme (Berlin: Carl Pataky, 1898) reprint, Bern: Herbert Lang, 1971.

August Sauer, Frauenbilder aus der Blütezeit der deutschen Literatur. Mit 15 Originalportraits (Leipzig: A. Titze, 1885) gives a romanticized view of women associated with great male authors.

Johannes Scherr, Geschichte der deutschen Frauenwelt. In drei Büchern nach den Quellen (Leipzig: Otto Wigand, 1864). This very popular, nationalistic interpretation of German history contains useful positivistic detail; while Scherr centers his attention too much on aristocratic women and deals primarily with idealized wives, mothers, and lovers of great poets in the chapter on "Frauen und Dichter," he has important chapters on women in the Reformation and on witch persecution.

Alwin Schultz, Das Alltagsleben einer deutschen Frau zu Anfang des 18. Jahrhunderts (Leipzig, 1890) is an impressionistic historical sketch of production, religion, and customs in the family of the self-sufficient household.

Those early twentieth century works on the same topics are the following:

Otto Heller, The German Woman Writer in the Nineteenth Century. Studies in Modern German Literature (Boston: Ginn, 1905).

Heinrich Spiero, Geschichte der deutschen Frauenwelt seit 1800 (Leipzig: B.G. Teubner, 1913).

Christine Touaillon, Der deutsche Frauenroman des 18. Jahrhunderts (Vienna and Leipzig: Wilhelm Braumüller, 1919).

Paul Kluckhohn, Die Auffassung der Liebe in der Literatur des 18. Jahrhunderts und in der deutschen Romantik (Tübingen: Max Niemeyer, 1922).

Else Hoppe, Liebe und Gestalt. Der Typus des Mannes in der Dichtung der Frau (Hamburg: Verlag der Frau, 1934).

[16] Elisabeth Friedrichs, Die deutsch-sprachigen Schriftstellerinnen des 18. und 19. Jahrhunderts. Ein Lexikon (Stuttgart: J.B. Metzler, 1981).

[17] Deutsche Dichterinnen vom 16. Jahrhundert bis zur Gegenwart, edited by Gisela Brinker-Gabler (Frankfurt: Fischer Taschenbuchverlag, 1978).

[18] Frauenfrage in Deutschland. Texte und Dokumente, edited by Elke Frederiksen (Stuttgart: Reclam, 1981, Book 7737).

[19] Sind das noch Damen? Vom gelehrten Frauenzimmer-Journal zum feministischen Journalismus, edited by Ruth-Esther Geiger and Sigrid Weigel (Munich: Frauenbuchverlag, 1981).

Martha Wallach

Ideal and Idealized Victims:
The Lost Honor of the Marquise von O., Effi Briest
and Katharina Blum in Prose and Film

I

Kleist's "The Marquise von O." was published in
1808, Fontane's Effi Briest in 1894 and Böll's The
Lost Honor of Katharina Blum in 1974. And yet, these
three prose works, each separated from the other by
about three quarters of a century, each featuring a
central character who is both victim and female, attracted the attention of some of the foremost movie-
makers of Europe in the seventies: Eric Rohmer, Rainer
Werner Fassbinder, Margarethe von Trotta and Volker
Schlöndorff. The three films derived from these works
have met with popular success as well as critical
acclaim.[1] Victimization is the common element in all
three which I would like to discuss. To what extent
is there an exploitation of the victim as victim, a
romanticization of her plight, and to what extent is
there criticism, an invitation to the audience to
analyze, to disapprove and to see alternatives?[2]

A brief discussion of the main characters of the
stories and the films based on them will precede a detailed analysis of the heroine as victim in The Lost
Honor of Katharina Blum. The final section of this
paper will compare the portrayal of all three heroines

"The Marquise von O." was written shortly before
Kleist's death and its heroine is a very Kleistian
character, the victim of mistaken identities, myster-
ious happenings, misunderstanding, unjust accusations
and the general "frail construction" of the world.
She is an innocent victim. To use an image from the
story: she is like the swan of the count's childhood
garden; although pelted with mud, she needs only to
dive to come up white again. First shown to us moved
by gratitude toward the dashing Russian officer who
saved her from rape by his men, she has no inkling
that he himself is guilty of the crime. Although an
adult with two children, she is completely subser-
vient to her parents and brother and allows her family to speak for her when her savior-rapist returns
with a marriage proposal. In heart-rending fashion

61

she pleads her innocence when they are outraged at
her claim that her pregnancy is a mystery to her.
When she is condemned by her parents, she asserts her
independence, however, by refusing to allow the family to take her children from her, establishing her
own household and disregarding convention with her
advertisement asking the child's father to step forward. When the Russian officer admits the deed, she
treats him as Satan incarnate and continues to reject
him despite a pro-forma marriage. He has to wait a
year to be forgiven and although she finally relents
and bears him many children, she has taken a stand --
at least for a while. The marriage restores her reputation, and Julietta, after her trials and tribula-
tions is again as white as the swan after the dive.

Eric Rohmer's film The Marquise von O. is quite
faithful to Kleist's script. Little has been added as
far as the text is concerned; but there are some
omissions and some changes of emphasis.[3] Interiors
and costumes are historically accurate and sparse,
colors are muted, there is a lot of white and light
green and the whole is often enveloped by a haze.
Many scenes suggest copper engravings of the period.
In keeping with this understatement the threat of im-
pending rape to which the Marquise is subjected is
also played down. Her "Zetergeschrei," as Kleist
calls it, is barely audible. Her savior from this
humiliation is introduced as a very forceful guardian
angel who literally leaps into the picture by scaling
a wall and leads the overwrought Marquise to the safety and privacy of another part of the castle. The
text barely hints at what happens next: "Hier - traf
er, da bald darauf ihre erschrockenen Frauen erschie-
nen,   Anstalten einen Arzt zu rufen; versicherte,
indem er sich den Hut aufsetzte,dass sie sich bald
erholen würde; und kehrte in den Kampf zurück."[4]
There is only a dash and the fact that he had removed
his hat to suggest that he came close to her. The
film adds "realistic" details. The Marquise is shown
in a private room, draped diagonally across a large
bed covered in red satin, still in a swoon. She is
wearing white satin. Count F. is shown in the door-
way looking longingly at her, while the scene is
bathed in a red glow from the fire.[5] This seductive
sight was captured on a poster advertising the film.
The many indications in the text that the Count has
a bad conscience after this, on the other hand, are
not made clear in the film. For example, Kleist tells

us that Count F. refuses to name the soldiers who at-
tacked the Marquise, he refuses to see her again and
accept her gratitude, his face becomes red when he is
praised for his "noble behavior" and he calls out:
"Julietta! Diese Kugel rächt dich!"[6] when he is supposedly mortally wounded. Kleist uses such indications, of course, to make the Count worthy of redemp-
tion and forgiveness. Not seeing them in the film
one is inclined to judge the Count more harshly despite the fact that he is shown yielding to overpower-
ing temptation.[7] The film romanticizes the incident
showing the Marquise in such an inviting pose and in
such luxurious surroundings which, we are encouraged
to believe, tempted the Count to violate her in her
unconscious state. The beauty and elegance of the
whole film tend to soften any indignation the viewer
might feel about the rape of Julietta, the white
swan. Thus the film is a very male fantasy.

In _Effi Briest_ Theodor Fontane depicts an ossi-
fied society in which maintaining one's social position and the outward appearance of honor are all-im-
portant. Effi subscribes to these values and is thus
a willing victim, despite her playfulness, her love
of danger and her impatience with many social conventions. Effi is victimized in a more socially ap-
roved manner than the Marquise von O. and accepts
her fate on the whole. She leaves her playmates to
hear Innstetten's marriage proposal, cheerfully goes
off on an educational honeymoon, bravely moves to a
remote Baltic outpost, manages fear and isolation
and "rebels" in secret by having a clandestine affair.
When this is discovered years later, she submits to
being cast out and having her child taken from her.
It is only when she realizes that her daughter is
being turned against her, that we see any open rebellion. When Effi dies of pneumonia and a broken
heart, she is again submissive, wanting her maiden
name on her gravestone, not to establish her independence from Innstetten, but because she has not
brought "honor" to her married name!

Fassbinder's black and white film adaptation
of _Effi_ is stylized and has a nostalgic quality with
luxurious interiors laden with ornamentation, lace
and mirrors. It is a stunning portrayal of the world
which is so important to Effi, which traps her and
destroys her. We are invited to contemplate and analyze Effi's fate through a series of distancing de-

vices, such as the old photo album effect achieved
by focusing on a group of people who pose as in an
old photograph, who slowly come to life only to freeze
again and fade to white as the scene ends. Quotes from
Fontane are read in a monotonous voice and mirrors
double the participants in a discussion. Hanna Schy-
gulla's Effi interpretation emphasizes the easily
seduced, luxury loving, ghost fearing, innocent, bored
aspects of the child bride. Her harsh scolding of
faithful Roswitha is startling and underscores the
oppression of the female servants who polish the
glitter of Effi's world Fassbinder's film is an in-
dictment of this world which made Effi's fate possible
and its stylized features are particularly effective
with an audience well acquainted with the novel.
Since he can build on this prior knowledge -- with
German audiences at least -- the stylized features
have a powerful effect and Fontane's more gentle
rebuke becomes almost scathing.[8]

Böll's portrayal of Katharina, the hard working
housekeeper and maid, emphasizes her difference from
others of her social station. She seeks solitude,
manages her money well and treasures her "Eigentums-
wohnung" and her car in which she enjoys long, soli-
tary drives. Her nickname, "the Nun," underscores the
departure from her former life which taking a young
man home from a masked ball represents. When he
turns out to be an army deserter unjustly suspected
of murder, this harboring of a "wanted criminal" and
her helping him escape, brings police and press to
her door and into her life full force. She does not
acquiesce. She lies to the police and continues to
hide her lover. When the publicity becomes unbearable
she shoots and kills the most offensive of the jour-
nalists. Katharina Blum is of course the heroine of
a novel written in the early seventies. She is un-
willing to bow her head in shame, to cooperate with
authority and to accept victimization. She lashes out
at her oppressors.

Margarethe von Trotta's and Volker Schlöndorff's
filmed version of The Lost Honor of Katharina Blum
introduces suspense by changing the order of events.
The film does not start with a murder which is then
explained to us; instead, we see Katharina dressed in
stark black and white at the masked ball, see her
fall in love with a stranger, witness the armed as-
sault on her apartment and watch her naked and exposed in the shower as the police ransack the place.

This nude addition to Böll's narrative made the cover
of Spiegel later, thereby proving Böll's point about
the exploitation of sex by the media. There are other
powerful visual effects the book could never give us:
Katharina contemplating her dead mother's body, Katharina looking at the obscene mail the publicity has
brought her, the onslaught of a huge contingent of
the German army on her lover's hide-away, the murder
scene, and the lovers embracing quickly while they are
being led through the corridors of the jail in which
they are to be confined at the end of the film. Katharina's victimization is being driven home to the audience in brilliant color. There is no question about
where the filmmakers want to direct our sympathies.
Böll's deliberately dry attempt at investigative
journalism has become a thriller with a serious and
passionately delivered message.

II

        Katharina Blum, the vulnerable victim of merci-
less persecution by police and press is an idealized
figure in several respects. Böll has given her many
qualities that have been traditionally valued very
highly by German culture and an additional set of
qualities generally found especially endearing in
women. The latter, in particular, make her an ideal
victim: defenseless, acquiescing and lovable. It is
this complex of characteristics that the Schlöndorff/
von Trotta film chooses to emphasize. The result is
that the victim is idealized further and that the
outrages to which she is subjected seem even more pernicious. The changes undertaken by the filmmakers to
this end will be discussed after an examination of
Katharina's specifically German and specifically female qualities.

        Traditionally high on any German value scale is
the concept of loyalty (Treue). Katharina is loyal
to Ludwig even when she discovers that he is a fugitive from justice; she helps him escape, provides his
hide-away and does not betray him to the police. She
has been a loyal employee throughout her career as
a maid, she continues to work even when an employer
is jailed, then visits him in jail. Despite her dislike of Sträubleder, she protects him during the police investigation by not mentioning his name, lying
about the origin of the envelope found in her apartment. By not disclosing the source of her intimate

knowledge of the utility tunnels in her building, she
also protects the architect of the building, Frau
Blorna, who by giving Katharina the architect's draw-
ings, makes Ludwig's escape possible. Katharina is incredibly hard working (fleissig). She works days at
the Blornas, nights and weekends at the Hierpertz'
and as a caterer. She is also very thrifty (sparsam),
living on next to nothing, saving money to pay off
her apartment as soon as possible. She is very well
organized (ordentlich). Her apartment is neat, the
records she keeps about her own and her employers'
expenses are precise. She has saved the Blornas from
the chaos that engulfed them before she started to
organize their household for them. Else Woltersheim
emphasizes her organizational skills in discussing
her career as a caterer.⁹ She seeks solitude and com-
plains that one cannot even find that in churches
nowadays (p. 413). Her long drives are motivated by
this search as well. She makes no compromises about
her social life. Although she enjoys dancing she
foregoes this pleasure because she does not like the
settings in which it takes place. She is absolute
in her insistence on mutual attraction and gentleness
in love relationships. Her divorce was motivated by
this insistence. She is serious. Her falling in love
with Ludwig Götten is characterized as "ernst und
feierlich" (p. 427). Frau Blorna cites her serious-
ness among the ideal qualities which make all men
fall in love with her: "nicht leichtfertig und doch...
liebesfähig, ernst und doch jung und so hübsch, dass
sie's selber nicht wusste" (p. 439). When she becomes an "accused," she is misunderstood, many of her
desirable qualities are believed to be hiding unsav-
ory aspects: her search for solitude during her long
drives is considered suspect. Her taking Götten home
makes her look promiscuous, whereas she is ordinarily
celibate. Her nickname "Nonne" when it is discovered,
is seen as evidence of obstreperousness (Sprödigkeit),
rather than a result of her vain search for tender-
ness (Zärtlichkeit). The things she acquired through
thrift and good planning are suspected of being ill-
gotten gains.

These qualities alone would make Katharina Blum
a heroine with which the German reading and viewing
public could identify, a heroine whose fall at the
hands of police and press would create outrage and a
heroine who commits a crime in the end because she
was too sorely tried, because like Michael Kohlhaas
she could not find justice anywhere. But Böll has

gone further still in "idealizing" Katharina. He makes
her an ideal victim, a female victim. The inspiration
for the novel was the case of a male victim, a professor in Hannover who gave shelter to Baader-Meinhof
people and who found his private life and his career
destroyed as a result of the ensuing publicity.[10]
And then there are Böll's own experiences with the
press after he published an article in Spiegel in
January 1972, blaming papers like Bild for the Baader-
Meinhof hysteria and asking for mercy and a fair trial
for Ulrike Meinhof. By transplanting the experiences
of an established professional in a high-prestige
profession and those of a famous writer onto the
shoulders of a young uninformed and politically unin-
terested person in a low prestige profession, Böll
already had a more pitiable and innocent victim; but
the effect is heightened by making that victim a woman and giving her qualities traditionally considered
lovable in women.

Katharina is naive, innocent and without guile.
Her motivations are pure, she is unaware of the cyni-
cism of others, unaware that she is breaking the law
in harboring a fugitive from justice and helping him
escape. Her police interrogator considers her "naiv
und ein bisschen zu romantisch" (p.416). The narrator
refers to her free discussion of Götten's phone call
as proof of her innocence (p. 431). She is in love
and no sacrifice is too great to bring for Ludwig.
This commitment supersedes all that has been important to her until now. Her co-operative attitude to
those in authority stops when it comes to Ludwig. She
is trusting. She takes a stranger home without even
knowing his last name. She tells her life's story
to the police in compulsive detail without suspecting
that it will all be in the paper tomorrow. She is
vulnerable. Blorna calls her "so verletzlich, so ver-
dammt verletzlich" (p.439). This keeps him from taking advantage of her, but most of her other employers
whom she has had to fend off since she was fourteen
years old were not so "considerate." She is weak in
some respects. Although she rejects Sträubleder's
advances, she does accept his ring and the key to his
villa. She allows the police to break in without pro-
testing their invasion of her privacy. She is mother-
ly toward Ludwig. She is concerned about his comfort
in his hide-away and when he is apprehended she is
relieved, because now he is protected from his own
foolhardy actions: "Sie zeigte sich erleichtert
darüber, dass Götten verhaftet sei, nun, sagte sie,

könne er keine Dummheiten mehr machen" (p. 454). She
allows others to take care of her. Blornas help finance her apartment, give her left-over food and, in
the film, hand-me-down clothes. Else Woltersheim,
her godmother, mothers her. As housekeeper, cook and
maid, she is in a helping profession par excellence.
She is helpful beyond the call of duty in attending
to the households of her employers, the Blornas and
the Hierpertzes. She also takes care of her family.
She provides her brother with pocket money while he
is in jail, despite his past financial exploitation
of her. She maintains her father's grave. She is
beautiful and yet unaware of it (p. 439). She has
good taste. Frau Woltersheim makes a point of her
capabilities in that respect and emphasizes her
"ästhetische Seite" (p. 424). She is neat in her personal appearance and the term "adrett" is applied
to her time and again. She provokes pity in reader
and viewer alike. The destruction of the private
life and reputation and even the very soul of this
wholesome exemplary and defenseless woman is truly
villainous and her final desperate revenge becomes
understandable and forgiveable.

The film tends to emphasize those qualities which
make Katharina an ideal victim. A series of changes
result in Katharina appearing shyer, younger, even
more wholesome and naive. There is a change of
clothes in her first appearance in the film. While
Böll had her depart for the carnival party at Else
Woltersheim's in honey-colored beige skirt and blouse,
with red stocking, red shoes and a red carnation in
her hair, Schlöndorff and von Trotta dress her in a
stark black skirt and white blouse. Not only does
this make her look more like a nun, but it also emphasizes her "Adrettheit" and makes her look younger
than her 27 years. It also seems very conservative
as does her bluish grey VW, which was red in the
story. A similar effect is achieved through her short,
white, terrycloth robe substituting for the green
robe with embroidered daisies of the text, which
she is wearing when the police break into her apartment (p.391/2).

Her victimization is intensified in the film
through such devices as police in riot gear descend-
ing upon her apartment, a shot going off while they
are searching the place and a view of Katharina
seen naked through the bathroom door having to submit
to an anal examination by the matron. In the novel,

on the other hand, there is no riot gear, no shot and
we are told only that Katharina had to dress without
being able to close the bathroom door completely
(p. 394). There is a later mention of "Leibesvisita-
tion" during which the key to Sträubleder's villa
had not been found, but we are not given any particu-
lars (p. 442). The film also adds the order Blorna's
associate Hack gives Katharina during the search of
her apartment when he tells her to dress because it
made a bad impression on his men to see her so scan-
tily clad. Here the victim of a raid is blamed for
her appearance when it is the police who have caught
her by surprise. This serves to dramatize the efforts
of police and press to turn poor, sweet, innocent
Katharina into a brazen hussy and terrorist gun moll.
Böll twice uses terms like "Triumph" and "triumphier-
end" in describing Katharina's attitude toward the
police when they break in (p.393). This was not evident in the film where Katharina seems more hesitant,
even frightened, vulnerable and embarassed. The film
also does not show her as "aufreizend gelassen an ihrer Anrichte lehnend" (p. 393). When Katharina is
introduced to us in the story the term "kühl" is used
several times to describe her: by her boss Blorna
when he describes her to the press as "kühl und klug,"
by others in the building when they are interviewed
by the police, by the doctor when her mother dies
(p. 452). This is not a quality which the film-Katharina conveys, she is too loving, too trusting to represent cool detachment. The film shows us Katharina's
cleanliness by introducing an almost compulsive clean-
ing scene. When Katharina is brought to her jail cell
and finds that someone has thrown up all over the
toilet she first cleans up the mess (which is shown
to us with a long and slow shot from behind Katharina's back) before she sits down on her cot with a
happy look on her face which could possibly be interpreted as housewifely satisfaction! Böll has her
wrinkle her nose and light up a cigarette in the
novel! While the latter conveys disdain and a devil-
may-care attitude, the former suggests "cleanliness
approaching Godliness," servitude and a turning of
the other cheek. Katharina does not smoke throughout
the film contributing to the image of clean living.
Her servitude is emphasized by her waiting on the
others at Blorna's after Ludwig has been apprehended,
while in the novel it is Frau Woltersheim who is
making the sandwiches while Katharina is being
spoiled for a change (p. 455).

Anyone seeing the film before reading the novel would no doubt be surprised to hear that others in the apartment building thought Katharina to be a "Chefsekretärin oder Abteilungsleiterin in einem Warenhaus" (p. 493). I would like to suggest that in the film she looks more like a "Abiturientin" or the graduate of a "Höhere Töchterschule," "arm, doch wohlerzogen." With her simple pageboy hairdo, with her black hand-me-down clothes (not counting the "Beduinenfrau" costume which she wears only briefly, she wears only three outfits: black skirt/white blouse; black skirt/beige and black home-made looking sweater; black sweater and skirt), with her modest, longer-than-fashionable-in-1974 skirt and sensible shoes she just does not look like someone who would be successful in the business world. A change in the film which adds to the impression of naiveté is the fact that she calls Ludwig on her aunt's tapped telephone and thus gives away his hiding place to the police while he admonishes her not to do it again, thus suggesting that he, being worldly-wise, suspects a bug. In the story he calls her; she does not even have his telephone number. And although she also does not expect a bug here, the reversal results in a changed emphasis. The film suggests a Katharina inexperienced with a gun; she winces each time she shoots Tötges. In the story we find out that Katharina had been a waitress for a "Schützenverein" where she had done quite a bit of shooting, she had gone to target practice with Else Woltersheim and her friend and had used the same gun before. She is specifically described as "eine gute Schützin" (p. 470). In the same vein, she asks Else's friend for the key to his apartment in the novel, presumably so she can get at the gun, while in the film it is offered to her, suggesting that she might have happened upon the gun as if by accident. In the novel there is mention of "entschlossene Kaltblütigkeit" on her part before the deed and lack of "Reue" afterwards (p. 455); neither is conveyed in the film. One could perhaps describe her as dazed when she is interrogated by Beizmenne after the murder.

The result of all these changes is a film-Katharina who is not only a victim but a martyr for love, destroyed by the relentless and completely undeserved attack by the police, the "Boulevardpresse" and the public. By emphasizing her innocence and trust, by making her look younger, more willing to serve others, more impulsive about shooting Tötges, less experi-

enced with a gun, the viewing public is ready to take
her to its heart, to forgive her taking the life of
someone who has so grievously wronged her. The cool
and detached story-Katharina has of course also been
taken to its heart by the reading public which is
aware of more fiendish practices of the ZEITUNG and
the police than could ever be conveyed in a film and
is therefore also ready to forgive, despite the suggestion that Tötges was "killed in cold blood." Many
of the changes the filmmakers made were dictated by
the medium: A complicated and analytical piece of
prose full of digressions, innuendos, suspicions,
different versions of the same incident, has been
turned into a thriller with the murder as a surprise
ending. There was need for drama, for strong visual
impressions and Katharina's transformation served
these ends -- in part. The changes also worked in the
direction of turning Katharina into an even more traditional, victimized, female figure: beautiful and
wronged, not unlike Effi, not unlike the Marquise
of O. It is a traditional character from which Margarethe von Trotta in her independent work has since
distanced herself. Christa Klages, for example, is
neither beautiful, nor particularly shy, nor particularly young or innocent. What motivates her is not
the romantic "love-at-first-sight" of a strange man,
but the needs of her kindergarten and a touch of
ennui. She is the fugitive from justice; men do the
harboring. She is a much more active heroine than her
film ancestor Katharina Blum.

Although the film changed much when it adapted
the story, it cannot be said that Schlöndorff/von
Trotta did violence to Böll's work. In an interview
in Die Zeit, they describe their cooperation with
Böll who sent them page proofs two months before
publication and wrote pages of additional dialogue
for them, inviting them to choose the sentences
they could use. All three together invented additional scenes.[11] Since this cooperation was so close and
the appearance of film and book almost simultaneous,
it could be said that Böll's work appeared in two
versions -- one film, one prose.

III

Effi and the Marquise are "ideal" victims by
virtue of their helplessnes and their dependence on

71

their parents who betray them at critical moments. Both women are devoted to and completely controlled by parents who pressure them into "suitable" marriages, reject them when scandal threatens or engulfs them and later forgive. Neither Effi nor the Marquise seem to resent this fickle parental support to any great extent. Both come back when their parents beckon. The Marquise briefly leaves the fold when her father seems to be shooting at her, only to return and be as controlled as ever by her family. Much could be made of her angry departure and the "schöne Anstrengung" which made her better acquainted with herself, but it cannot be overlooked that she defers even more to her parents after her return. The reply to her advertisement seems more promising to her because the writer has requested to meet her in her parents' house rather than in her own; her father makes a marriage contract with the Count without her request or consent; her mother starts inviting the Count after he has given a large sum of money to the child and made a will leaving his fortune to the Marquise, although the latter is not speaking to him at this point. Effi allows her parents to manipulate her into a far too early marriage with her mother's former beau for the sake of rank and social station; she accepts her mother's censure and is grateful when she is later allowed to return and end her days at home.

The Marquise and Effi are "idealized victims" in that they are shown as good women who do not deserve their fate. The Marquise, a shy, upright widow, who reads and paints, brings up her children well in rural solitude and has difficulty making up her mind, had no intentions to remarry. She is filled with gratitude and completely trusts her savior who betrays her trust. While it is true that Kleist shows her physically attracted to the Count, it cannot be said that she "wanted to be raped," as some interpreters have suggested.[12] Effi is idealized through her beauty, her childlike naiveté; she is wronged by her parents who push her into a teenage marriage and by her much older husband who attempts to control her with fear. She is no match for her experienced and cynical seducer. The pity viewer and reader alike feel for both women is also increased through the very great height of privilege from which they fall.

In both their prose and film existence, the Marquise, Effi and Katharina, so widely separated by

time, temperament, literary style and social context,
share a typically female fate: loss of sexual honor
and its attendant loss of "good repute." It is im-
posed upon the Marquise from without and her fall
from grace is reversed -- superficially at least. Effi
and Katharina take the initial steps themselves and
for them there is no return. In each case the censure
of society is out of all proportion to the "crime"
and in the case of the Marquise it is directed
toward the victim rather than the offender. Kleist/
Rohmer show us a "happy end" in which the victim for-
gives and marries the offender. Fontane/Fassbinder
end their tale with the death of both seducer and
seduced while Böll/von Trotta/Schlöndorff imprison
their lovers. Punishment is thus meted out more
justly in Effi and Katharina Blum while the Marquise
has to swallow her pride and is not allowed a quest
for justice in the style of Michael Kohlhaas. While the
filmed Marquise romanticizes and thus belittles the
protagonist's plight, the filmed Effi and Katharina
invite criticism of a society in which honor is lost
so unjustly and its loss punished so severely.[13]

University of Wisconsin
at Green Bay

Notes

[1] For a detailed analysis of the adaptation of
these films, see Modern European Filmmakers and the
Art of Adaptation, ed. Andrew S. Horton and Joan
Magretta (New York: Ungar, 1981). For general
treatments of film adaptations, see George Bluestone,
Novels into Film (Berkeley: University of California
Press, 1957); Robert Richardson, Literature and Film
(Bloomington: Indiana University Press, 1969); Marie-
Claire Ropars-Wuilleumier, De la Littérature au Cin-
éma: Genèse d'une Écriture (Paris: Armand Colin,
1970); Geoffrey Wagner, The Novel and the Cinema
(Cranbury, N.J.: Fairleigh Dickinson University Press,
1975). For a discussion of the New German Cinema,
see John Sandford, The New German Cinema (New York:
Da Capo Press, 1980); New German Critique, special
double issue on new German cinema, Nos. 24-25 (Fall-
Winter 1981-82), ed. David Bathrick and Miriam
Hansen.

[2] Although not specifically treating the films under discussion here, an excellent work on the portrayal of women in film is E. Ann Kaplan, Women and Film: Both Sides of the Camera (New York: Methuen, 1983); contains bibliography.

[3] One such change of emphasis is the telling of the swan story in two parts. The second part is not told until the end of the film, which emphasizes its "happy-end" aspects and makes the end less of a compromise and more of a "rebirth."

[4] Heinrich von Kleist, "Die Marquise von O...: Nach einer wahren Begebenheit, deren Schauplatz vom Norden nach dem Süden verlegt worden," Werke in einem Band, Hanser Klassiker Volksausgabe (München: Carl Hanser, 1966), p. 659.

[5] Another realistic detail is the sleeping potion the Marquise receives, so that it is easier for the audience to believe that she really does not know who the father is. See Alan Spiegel, "The Cinematic Text: Rohmer's The Marquise of O... (1976) from the story by Heinrich von Kleist," Modern European Filmmakers and the Art of Adaptation, ed. Andrew S. Horton and Joan Magretta (New York: Ungar, 1981), p. 322.

[6] Kleist, p. 661.

[7] Alan Spiegel, after calling attention to the fact that "the count leaves, waits, then returns later that evening to satisfy his desire," says about this deliberate act: "Rohmer's hero is more calculating and self-conscious than Kleist's." Modern European Filmmakers, p. 322.

[8] For an analysis of Fassbinder's work, see Fassbinder, ed. Tony Rayns (London: British Film Institute, 1979); Also Rainer Werner Fassbinder, Reihe Film 2, ed. Peter W. Jansen and Wolfram Schuette (München: Carl Hanser, 1982).

[9] Heinrich Böll, "Die verlorene Ehre der Katharina Blum: Oder wie Gewalt entsteht und wohin sie führen kann," Heinrich Böll Werke: Romane und Erzählungen 5 1971-1977 (Köln: Kiepenheuer and Wietsch, 1978), p. 423. All further references are to this edition and are given in the text.

[10] For a more detailed account, see Heinrich Böll: Freies Geleit für Ulrike Meinhof, ed. Frank Gruetzbach (Köln: Kiepenheuer and Wietsch, 1972).

[11] Wolf Donner, "Sieben Fragen an Volker Schlöndorff und Margarethe von Trotta," Die Zeit, "Kritik und Information," No. 42, 17 October, 1975, p. 15, cols. 1-4.

[12] For example, Günter Blöcker,   Heinrich von Kleist oder Das absolute Ich, 2nd ed. (Berlin: Argon Verlag, 1960), p. 178.

[13] For valuable suggestions I would like to thank my colleagues Jeanette Clausen, Heinz Geppert and Ken Fleurant; thanks are also due to Marjorie Tussing, who chaired the Women in German MLA section on film, where this paper was presented, December 1982 in Los Angeles.

Anna K. Kuhn

Margarethe von Trotta's Sisters:
Interiority or Engagement?

Margarethe von Trotta is well known to followers
of the New German Cinema. Like Rainer Werner Fassbinder, von Trotta has had a multifaceted cinematic career. As an actress, von Trotta worked with Fassbinder,
Reinhard Hauff, Claude Chabrol, and Volker Schlöndorff.
Under the tutelage of Schlöndorff, whom she married in
1971, von Trotta has also developed her directorial
skills. To date she has coscripted five films with
Schlöndorff: The Sudden Wealth of the Poor People of
Kombach (1971), A Free Woman (Strohfeuer, 1972), The
Lost Honor of Katharina Blum (1975), Coup de Grace
(1976), and Circle of Deceit (1981); she also codirect-
ed Katharina Blum.

Since her debut as sole director of The Second
Awakening of Christa Klages in 1977, von Trotta has
become the leading woman filmmaker of contemporary
German cinema. Christa Klages portrays female solidarity between two unlikely candidates: the rebellious
critic of bourgeois capitalist society, Christa Klages,
who robs a bank in order to rescue a kindergarten
threatened with financial ruin, and a prototypical
servant of capitalist society, a bank teller, witness
to the robbery.

In Christa Klages, von Trotta uses paradigms of
the suspense thriller to generate audience expectations which she then disappoints. The surprise conclusion, in which the bank teller's obsession with Christa, her stalking of her prey, is shown to arise out of
admiration rather than out of a sense of reprisal,
shocks both the audience and Christa. The bank teller's
refusal to identify Christa to the police reveals her
as an unexpected ally. The solidarity evinced on the
part of the teller underscores the feminist message
of the film.

Von Trotta's third film, Marianne and Julianne
(Die bleierne Zeit, 1981), also has an explicit political theme: terrorism. But this film, while it also
explores the relationship between two women, does so
from a different perspective. The two women of the
title are sisters, one who rebels and one who does
not, and the film treats their relationship as much
as the politics of terrorism.

77

Sisters or the Balance of Happiness (1979), von Trotta's second film, initially appears to be a personal family history, the story of a relationship between two women which is essentially devoid of social and political resonance. Here, as in Christa Klages, von Trotta works with inversion. By playing with motifs of German Romanticism, she creates expectations of the extreme subjectivity devoid of political ramifications which characterizes this most subjective literary movement. But here again, expectations are overturned, and what seemed exclusively personal takes on broader political meaning. Instead of being an anomaly in her work, Sisters shows on closer examination the same sets of concerns, in a different constellation, as her two other films.

Sisters, a portrayal of the symbiotic relationship between the siblings Maria and Anna, is reminiscent of Ingmar Bergman's introspective studies of feminine interaction. The opening sequence of the film, the progressively darkening approach shot of a forest, immediately establishes the introverted tone of the film. Having both an expositional and symbolic function, the forest shot, inextricably linked to the figure of Anna, helps furnish the personal history of the sisters. The initial mute image of this forest (which occurs again after Anna's suicide, thus essentially framing her story) is soon augmented by the voice-over of the young Maria. Cutting to a shot of the two children in bed, the camera shows a self-assured Maria sovereignly reading from a book of fairy tales to a cowering Anna, who hangs on her every word while writhing in fear at her side. The content of the fairy tale Maria is reading, the story of children lost in the woods, clearly has significance for the sisters as well: it serves as a metaphor for their psychic states.

Thus this sequence establishes the experiential communality of the siblings and articulates the power relationship so crucial to the film's subtitle. The balance of happiness is sustained as long as both siblings retain the big sister, leader-protector (Maria) and the follower, admirer-protected (Anna) roles paradigmatically shown in the opening sequence. When, however, the leadership role of the older sister, natural in childhood, gives way to the dominance of the adult Maria, and the dependent

Anna rebels against this oppression, the balance of happiness is upset.

The forest sequence, with its transition from light to dark, is also symbolic of the journey into the recesses of the psyche upon which the film will embark. As such, it becomes an emblem of the film's interiority.

Using acoustic elements as a bridge (the voice-over continues reading the fairy tale), von Trotta brings the action into the present by cutting to a shot of the sleeping Anna, sprawled over her cluttered desk, arms extended, wrists up in what amounts to an adumbration of her suicide position. She then cuts to a shot of Anna's pet lizard, which, together with the forest, becomes the leitmotiv of the vulnerable, troubled younger sister.

Like the forest shot, the lizard appears three times and becomes identified with Anna's inner life. In one of the film's most powerful sequences, a closeup of the lizard marks the transition to Anna's realm. A recording of Purcell's Dido and Aeneas serves as the acoustic background of this scene. Against the hauntingly melancholic sounds of "Dido's Lament" ("Remember Me"), we watch a desperate, angst-ridden Anna struggle to sustain her sense of self. In quick succession, the alienated Anna takes three photos of herself, hoping without success to find in them or in the reflection in the mirror into which she stares some reaffirmation of self. The closing shot with a sobbing Anna standing in the middle of the room, embracing herself and rocking to and fro, is testimony to her failure, to her loss of identity.

In this sequence, the acoustic and the visual components join to evoke a sense of foreboding. Given the fact that "Dido's Lament" is her death song and immediately precedes her suicide, and given the inconsolable image of Anna in the closing shot, the scene serves as a foreshadowing of Anna's suicide.

The connection between Anna, the lizard, and interiority is made even more explicit in the sequence which shows a closeup of Anna standing behind the lizard's tank, face pressed to the glass, staring pensively at the animal. Coming forth from behind the tank, she stares at Maria for a moment, then articulates with great insight the dynamics of their mutually dependent relationship: "Du brauchst mich, damit ich dich brauche."

Just as the lizard is confined in a glass tank, so Anna is entrapped in the apartment she shares with her sister. With great acumen, von Trotta establishes the respective milieux of the sisters as the spatial correlative of their characters and psychological states. Thus the crisp, efficient Maria, the stronger, more independent, more aggressive of the two sisters, is shown against the backdrop of the functional modern office in which she works as an executive secretary in order to support her sister's studies. Maria's professional persona, her no-nonsense, businesslike efficiency, stands in sharp contrast to the exotic disarray of Anna's sphere. The strictly functional, barren office in which she spends the vast majority of her time mirrors the barrenness of Maria's emotional life. Maria is the coolly self-assured, totally competent, indispensable secretary who unquestioningly carries out the duties assigned her by her high-powered, cold-blooded, industrialist boss. If she initially appears to be intensely masculine, closer examination reveals that Maria's power in the workplace lies in fulfilling the stereotypically feminine nurturing role. Maria is the angel, not in the house but in the office, serving, ministering to the needs of the male.

In depicting the character of Anna, von Trotta turns to another stereotype: that of the dependent, helpless female. In contrast to her outwardly, i.e., professionally, well-adjusted sister, Anna is at variance with her professional environment. If Maria's realm emanates orderliness and rationality, then Anna's sphere points to her romantic, troubled nature. A biology student who questions the meaning of DNA research, she is no longer able to accept the validity of what she is being taught. She suffers from the discrepancy between the acutely cerebral, sophisticated scientific research on gene manipulation and the inability to deal with the basic human emotion of love. Unlike Maria, Anna is incapable of superficial interaction with her fellow students. While empathetic toward others (as in the scene with the blind woman), she is incapable of forming other relationships (as shown by the scene with the male student in the lobby). Hence she becomes increasingly more withdrawn and disturbed.

In Anna's dealings with Maria, powerlessness becomes power. Through her dependence on Maria, she plays upon her sister's nurturing instincts and manipulates her into ministering to her and into protecting her. In establishing that the pathological interaction between the siblings is predicated on the acting out of stereotypically female roles, von Trotta calls into question these roles.

As long as the sisters' private personae are totally absorbed by their intense relationship, they are able to sustain (albeit with some difficulty, some of which seems ritualized) a balance in their relationship. The submissive-dominant balance of their mutually dependent relationship becomes irreconcilably upset, however, when the boss's son Maurice becomes interested in Maria. His attentions cause the passive-aggressive Anna to become openly hostile and eventually self-destructive.

Since Anna's identity is inextricably intertwined with Maria, it follows that the threat posed by the attentions of Maurice to the latently incestuous relationship between the sisters must strain Anna's already unstable psyche. It is hardly fortuitous that Anna commits suicide on the night that Maria consummates her affair with Maurice. Anna's suicide is the final, violent power play of the impotent.

If Anna is the main vehicle of interiority in the first part of the film, after her death she bequeaths this propensity to Maria. In a section of her diary dedicated specifically to Maria, Anna informs her sister that she has killed herself on her (Maria's) account, that Maria was the target of her death. In a ghoulish description of what amounts to vampire exorcism, Anna admonishes Maria to put a stone on her grave, a stake through her heart, to chop off her hand, in order to prevent her rising up and haunting her, to prevent her avenging herself on her sister.

Anna's diary entry: "Den Traum, den ich mir

vom Leben machte, raubte mir das Leben," signals the shift which the theme of interiority will take. In the latter half of the film, dreams play an increasingly important role. Made susceptible both by the formidable power of suggestion of Anna's dedication and by her own guilt, Maria is soon haunted by Anna-- in her dreams.

In the first role-reversed dream sequence, von Trotta visually reasserts the sisters' symbiosis. In what appears to be a replay of Maria's discovery of Anna's body, we see a figure walk to the threshold of a room. The cut to the body presents us as viewers with the full violence of the suicide. As Maria's psychic projection, it is however not the body of Anna, but that of Maria with which we are confronted. In lieu of Maria's horrified reaction, we see Anna's smug smile. Thus the sequence can be interpreted not merely as Maria's awareness that with Anna, a part of herself has died, but also, in keeping with Freud's theory of wish fulfillment, as a death wish on Maria's part.

As with Anna, the interiority (dream) sequences document the rise of anxiety and the dissolution of self in Maria. The second dream sequence presents us with an unsettled Maria, who, turning fearfully as a door behind her eerily opens, finds herself confronted with a horror-film-like white Anna noisily eating (another reminder of vampire motifs). The horror-film atmosphere is sustained in the final dream sequence, in which Maria, looking into a mirror, sees the reflection of the back of a figure. Von Trotta again underscores the interdependence of Maria and Anna by having the figure turn to present a profile, revealing Anna dressed in Maria's clothes.

Had von Trotta restricted herself to a depiction of the interaction of the two siblings, one would have to classify her film under the contemporary movement of New Subjectivity. She broadens the parameters of the film's appeal, however, by extending her definition of sisterhood and by redefining the concept of family through the figure of Mariam, a young secretary in Maria's firm who assumes an increasingly important role in Maria's life after Anna's suicide. Despite Mariam's romantic interest in the boss's son, her response upon learning of the developing relationship between him and Maria is one of solidarity. ("Die Hauptsache

ist, dass er in eine von uns verliebt ist.") After
Anna's suicide, Mariam offers herself as a daughter
to the sisters' mother, thereby fulfilling a role
that Maria, weighed down by family history, can no
longer play.

Like the bank teller in Christa Klages, whose
consciousness is raised over the course of the film
until, by not identifying Christa, she affirms feminist solidarity, Mariam serves as a yardstick in
Sisters. Conceived as a counterpoint to Anna and
Maria, the feisty Mariam is a truly independent,
self-determining figure who refuses to grant power
over her life to anyone. By introducing Mariam as
an alternative, von Trotta repudiates the stereotypical female roles embodied by the sisters. Upon
discovering Anna's diary and realizing the full
extent of Maria's pathology, Mariam refuses to allow
Maria to manipulate her into assuming Anna's submissive role. Mariam's successful, self-affirming
rebellion stands in sharp contrast to Anna's self-
destructive, desperate act. In a scene reminiscent
of Fassbinder's Petra von Kant, von Trotta has
Mariam leave. An abandoned, lonely Maria must now
balance the account of her life (as the subtitle,
both in German and English, indicates).

The introduction of Mariam also serves to make
the political ramifications of Maria's behavior explicit. Maria's attempt to duplicate her relationship with Anna by having Mariam move in and by paying
for her training as a translator makes clear that
her relationship to these women is predicated on
the capitalist structure. By paying for their studies, she attempts to buy their allegiance. While von
Trotta's portrayal of Maria's manipulation of in-
terpersonal relationships in this case is explicitly anti-capitalist, her criticism is generally
more broad-based. The film presents us with a
critique of a culture in which the outwardly successful are those who have stifled their own subjectivity and who attempt to stifle it in others as
well.

Thus, despite its personal themes, despite the
importance of the theme of interiority, Sisters
ultimately offers an engaged perspective by exam-
ining the stunted personalities of Maria and Anna,
both of whom are cast in stereotypical feminine

roles (self-sacrificing martyr and submissively dependent woman). By pointing out the psychic cost and emotional ravages wrought by these roles, von Trotta is making a political statement. Though the film restricts itself to personal relationships, the personal has here become the political.

The problematic of subjectivity serves as a unifying element between the personal and the political. By disallowing Anna's subjectivity, by foisting upon her sister her own image of her, Maria duplicates male-female relationships. In its study of Maria and Anna, the film shows that the relationships between two women can be as power-oriented and freedom-limiting as that between a man and a woman. In the figure of Anna, on the other hand, von Trotta shows the dangers of unbridled subjectivity. In addition to their family bonding, a lack of self-awareness and identity binds these truncated personalities to each other. Self-knowledge and autonomy are unattainable for the sisters within the confines of their relationship.

Ironically, it is Mariam's self-assertive rejection of Maria that is responsible for the tone of quiet optimism with which the film ends. For Maria, who resolves to continue Anna's diary entries, there remains the possibility of developing into a three-dimensional, fully integrated personality -- "ich will Maria und Anna sein" -- through self-awareness and inwardness -- "ich will lernen zu träumen, während ich lebe." The closing shot of Maria opening Anna's diary, about to embark on the process of getting in touch with herself, holds promise.

University of Pennsylvania

Barbara Drygulski Wright

The Feminist Transformation of
Foreign Language Teaching

Around 1959 or '60, when I first began to learn
German in high school, my German teacher insisted
upon using a textbook from before the second world
war. She did so because in that text all the German
passages were printed in the Gothic alphabet, and
she wanted us all to learn to read it easily. While
I don't recall the book containing anything politically objectionable, it was distinctly different from the more "modern" foreign language textbooks then coming into favor. Instead of following
some young American around on his clean-cut, faintly
romantic adventures (and I say "his" in the specific,
not the generic sense, because the central character was invariably male), we read animal fables
and snippets of 19th century poetry. We learned a
considerable vocabulary for birds and beasts, woods
and meadows, weather and the animal cares of the
barnyard. I remember experiencing a distinct shock
one day when my teacher brought in a German women's
magazine, a rather elegant, glossy affair with ex-
quisite-looking models. I was shocked to realize,
first that living people used this language at all;
and second, that the people who used it certainly
did not look like the trolls, woodcutters and peas-
ants I had grown accustomed to. Now obviously, as
a reasonably intelligent fifteen-year-old I knew,
rationally at least, that Germany was a modern in-
dustrial nation and so on. But the shock I experienced was real nevertheless, and the memory of
it is vivid in me still, because the subliminal
message of six months' study with that text had been
so powerful.

Thus when feminists in the early 70s began to
look at textbooks with a newly raised consciousness
and to object to the unwelcome lessons such textbooks taught, their arguments made eminently good
sense to me. However, in the foreign languages as
in other disciplines, the feminist critique of traditional methods and materials has changed and evolved
over the last decade, becoming increasingly more
sophisticated and sensitive to more subtle problems of imbalance, more inclusive of feminist
ideals. The evolution of a feminist perspective in

foreign language teaching has not occured in isolation but rather has developed in partnership with women's studies scholarship across the liberal arts, and it is this evolution of feminist thinking about foreign language instruction that I would like to trace in this paper. Three phases can be distinguished in this development: at first, a primary focus on images of women and girls in textbooks; then a broadening of concern to include women's place in the target culture; and finally, a critical look at the very language itself that we are teaching and at the value judgments which inform our decisions to include or exclude certain semantic and syntactic possibilities. Or we can describe this development another way. That is, the attention of feminists has shifted from issues of sexism and bias (or negative treatment of women) to equity (or a more positive revaluation of women's roles, particularly in culture) to a profound rethinking of what we teach and how. In any case, since our problems with textbooks even at the simplest level are far from solved, each of these successive phases has not supplanted but rather supplemented earlier concerns.

The first phase of feminist concern with teaching materials began around 1970 and peaked in 1977 or '78. During this period numerous books and articles appeared, in everything from the popular presses to highly specialized professional journals, detailing the discriminatory treatment of girls and women in standard teaching materials and arguing that this bias worked to the disadvantage of male as well as female students. Education, after all, was supposed to expand the individual's options for personal development, not constrict them; rigid stereotyping, however, limited everyone's choices. Feminists within professional societies began to form caucuses, and at regional and national conferences they organized sessions devoted to the problem of sexist bias in their teaching materials. These sessions drew heavy attendance and sometimes even received press coverage. Checklists were developed to help everyone from the individual instructor to an entire school district in the assessment of bias. The checklists produced data that could be used in a number of ways: the data helped schools and departments to decide for or against purchase of certain texts; it indicated clearly to teachers where they must compensate when faced with an objectionable text; and it could be used by parents and teachers when they wrote letters of protest to publishing houses. Publishers, in response to pressure both within their organizations and in the marketplace, issued guidelines designed to help authors and editors avoid offensive treatment not only of women and girls, but also of minorities and disadvantaged groups such as the elderly or handicapped.

During this period, work in foreign language circles paralleled the work done across the entire spectrum of American education, from kindergarten through post-secondary schooling and in many different disciplines. It was significant and valuable work because it helped to translate the issue of bias into the specific idiom of the foreign language classroom. Feminist efforts affected the high school, but they tended to concentrate on the college level and to have a special urgency there: because so much foreign language instruction in this country takes place at colleges and universities; because foreign language curricula tend to be more heavily enrolled by women than men; and because foreign language competency is traditionally an essential component of a liberal arts education. For language instructors, feminism in the academy meant not theory or research but rather practical actions that would enable them to better serve both their students and the educational ideals of their institutions. The talks that were delivered on sexism and bias, the articles that were published and the checklists that were developed -- all reflect a basic concern with practical application.

Before we can review foreign language teachers' critiques of existing materials and their recommendations, however, we need to clarify what it is that foreign language textbooks are supposed to accomplish. Even this attempt at clarification, however, demonstrates how closely interwoven, indeed almost inextricable, necessary and gratuitous lessons may be. A foreign language textbook -- at least the sort in common use in this country -- has two basic functions to fulfill: first, it must teach the target language itself; and second, it must teach something of the culture or cultures in which that language is used.

Teaching the target language means teaching

grammar, vocabulary and usage. Grammatical phenomena are not really open to much discussion, although of course definitions of what is grammatically acceptable can and do change over time when a need arises. Many grammatical phenomena involve either natural or grammatical gender. One obvious example is gender-marking, which is far more pervasive in the commonly taught foreign languages than it is in English. The fact that gender-marking occurs in a language does not in itself constitute sexist bias; it is simply a grammatical necessity. However, foreign language textbooks have tended to introduce masculine forms first, to present feminine forms as deviations or derivatives of the masculine form, and to use masculine forms far more frequently in examples or drills. These and similar practices do represent bias.

When students learn vocabularly, they inevitably learn feminine and masculine pronouns, nouns and adjectives to describe female and male persons, appropriate titles and the names of various occupations. Sometimes the presence or absence of a word in the target language's lexical system reflects long-standing assumptions about women and men, just as in English we have "career woman" but no "career man" (except in the specialized context of the armed forces) and "family man" but no "family woman." Other words, for example those describing physical appearance or personality, may be neutral in themselves but become problematic because of the context in which they are repeatedly used. Occupations may be taught in the masculine or feminine form according to stereotypical notions of appropriate male and female employment -- either on the whim of the author or because the non-traditional form simply does not exist.

And third, students are supposed to learn usage -- what is idiomatic and"sounds good" in the target language. In this instance we are dealing with a question of linguistic habit, of preference, rather than with the basic grammatical structure of the language itself. For example, a language may prefer one past tense over another in normal conversation. Similarly, there is a tendency in the commonly taught European languages to use masculine forms not only specifically but generically, to stand for all human beings, female and male alike. Because gender-marking is more pervasive in these languages

than it is in English, the cumulative effect of this
generic masculine is even more devastating than it
is in English. Yet usage, like vocabulary and even more
than grammar, is also susceptible to change when the
need arises.

The second basic function of a foreign language
textbook is to teach culture. The book may teach
elite culture: the "great" individuals and "high
points" of the nation's historical or artistic tradition. Or the book may teach everyday culture: the
customs, assumptions, values and amusements of
everyday life. Most foreign language textbooks today
teach a combination of the two. Textbooks teach culture in two ways: explicitly, in reading passages,
dialogues, and other texts that convey information
while illustrating specific linguistic phenomena; and
implicitly or subliminally. These implicit or subliminal messages can be sent in a variety of ways. For
example, the very mix of materials that are included
or excluded will shape students' impressions of
what is important or inconsequential in the target
culture. Attitudes or information may be conveyed
in sections of the textbook that ostensibly serve
other purposes, such as grammar exercises or games
and activities. And personality traits, value judgments or the behavior of characters in the text, if
left unremarked, may well be interpreted by the
student as typical or at least acceptable.

Thus when a couple of authors sit down to write
a textbook, they face myriad decisions which are at
once both practical and ideological. Beginning in
the early 1960s, with the popularization of an
audio-lingual approach to language teaching, authors
and publishers devoted a good deal of thought to
method; the philosophical implications of these textbooks went largely unchallenged, however, until 1974.
In that year, at the annual meeting of the American
Association of Teachers of German held in the Federal Republic, Anneliese Sartori-Stein delivered a talk
entitled "Kultureller Chauvinismus im Grammatik-
Drill."[1] In it, she identified a number of "chauvin-
isms" and prejudicial attitudes that she had observed in German textbooks published in the US. The
books tended to focus on West Germany to the exclusion
of other German speaking countries, particularly
the German Democratic Republic. They assumed conflict between students and instructors and por-

trayed students as lazy, instructors as boring disciplinarians. They perpetuated a variety of
national clichés, and they reinforced the notion that
German was a particularly difficult language. In
their pages most social classes were ignored, except
for an educated upper-middle class of surgeons, professors and businessmen.

Last but certainly not least, Sartori-Stein
criticized the treatment of women in the seventeen
textbooks she examined. She found an obsession with
women's physical appearance, whereas men tended to be
described in terms of their profession or their intelligence. Women were repeatedly stereotyped as
gossipy busybodies, over-anxious mothers or fanatical
housekeepers. Unmarried women were portrayed as above
all interested in finding a husband. Even if a woman
worked outside the home, that work took second place
to her marital status and domestic responsibilities.
However, Sartori-Stein argued that German men in
these texts also suffered from sex stereotyping. They
were pressed into the role of stern, authoritarian
pater familias, reckless driver or helpless child in
need of mothering. In closing, Sartori-Stein called
upon teachers to be sensitive to such bias, to teach
"against" the text, and to demand that publishers
pay more attention to the content of their texts.
Otherwise, she warned, German teachers stood to lose
the next generation of students, a more sophisticated
and critical generation that would be repelled by the
perpetuation of blatant cultural clichés and preju-
dices.

At the Central States Conference on Foreign
Language Education the following year, Betty Schmitz
looked at "Sexism in French Language Textbooks" and
developed the four categories of bias -- exclusion,
subordination, distortion and degradation -- that
have proven so useful in evaluations of teaching
materials since then.[2] The category of exclusion includes both invisibility and underrepresentation of
women and girls. It refers to the proportion of a
book's contents devoted to females and males, and it
can be applied to virtually all the sections of a
standard textbook. In other words, in looking at
everything from dialogues, readings, comprehension
questions and recombination materials to grammar
explanations, exercises, pattern drills and illustrations, we can ask whether there are as many females
as males, whether feminine pronouns occur as often

as masculine ones, and whether generic masculine repeatedly renders the women in mixed groups invisible. Looking at the situation in 1975, Schmitz found that male characters outnumbered females by a ratio of 3 or 4 to 1; in illustrations, there were more than twice as many male central figures as female central figures.

Subordination refers to the tendency, again in all contexts, to portray women in a position of inferiority or dependency vis-à-vis the men in the textbook. When women are present, are they limited to supporting roles, or do they also figure as main characters with prestigious jobs? Are women shown outside of the domestic setting, or do we meet them as the wives, mothers or romantic interests of male characters? When professions are taught, are women portrayed in the same wide range of jobs as men, from low-paid ones to very prestigious ones? Schmitz asked these questions, and the answers were dismaying. She concluded that the analysis of the roles of women in the textbooks greatly qualified the original statistics on their presence. When women were present at all, they were limited to low-paid work. They appeared as stewardesses, nurses, secretaries, mothers, or nothing at all.

By distortion, Schmitz meant the stereotyping of intellectual abilities, personal characteristics, physical appearance, social status, domestic roles, professional ambitions and other factors according to sex. Male/female stereotyping, she observed, often took the form of complementary behavioral oppositions. Thus men might be presented as active, independent and strong while women appeared as passive, dependent and emotional. When Schmitz analysed the behavior exhibited by male and female characters in dialogues, readings and illustrations, and noted the descriptive adjectives used to refer to men and to women, she found marked sex-role stereotyping. Female characters were valued for their looks, while male characters were valued for their intelligence or skill. Males solved problems, gave help, travelled, participated in sports, engaged in conversations ranging from the trivial to the serious, used initiative and made plans or gave suggestions. Females, by comparison, solicited help rather than giving it, participated in social activities, performed routine and repetitive tasks such as shopping and self-care, engaged in trivial conversation, depended on others and expressed emotion or feeling.

The category of degradation, finally, referred to condescending statements or derogatory generalizations made about women. Schmitz examined French textbooks to see whether they contained examples of culturally condoned antifeminist attitudes or "girl-watching." She found women were not only excluded, reduced to subordinate roles, and portrayed in a distorted manner, but also subjected to degrading statements. Female characters were often perceived as unpleasant if they were too intelligent and an inconvenience if they were stupid or flighty. In analysing a textbook, Schmitz recommended that the reviewer be on the alert for statements that refer to women as: a danger or useless complication; bitchy, meddlesome, or manipulative; usually late or otherwise irresponsible; illogical, emotional, inept, or too intelligent for their own good; silly, stupid, childish or "cute"; and valued primarily for looks.

In closing, Schmitz was careful to explain that she was not recommending textbooks be revised to present an artificial statistical equality; nor should the cultural accuracy of male and female roles in various societies be violated. She argued, "It would be ridiculous to show 50 percent women students at the École Polytechnique. But it would not be ridiculous to include a reading about the first woman admitted to the École Polytechnique, or the first woman pilot in France." She called for textbooks that would reflect the variety of real life, instead of perpetuating stereotypes and attitudes that limited the personal development of both female and male students. To help remedy the existing situation, she recommended teacher awareness training: workshops to show teachers how to compensate for racism and sexism in teaching materials; pressure on school boards to review current or prospective teaching materials for sexist and racist bias; and writing letters to authors and publishers.

Although it was not one of the main points in her talk, Betty Schmitz implied that sexism in teaching materials was undesirable because it interfered with an accurate presentation of French women and men's lives. This argument was greatly strengthened with the appearance in 1977 of Thérèse Bonin and

Judith Muysken's excellent article, "French Women in Language Textbooks: Facts or Fiction?"[3] The first half of the article described the way women were typically portrayed in French language textbooks. In the second half of the article, this picture of French women was unmasked as a fiction having precious little correlation to the actual educational status, employment rates, self-image or aspirations of French women and girls. Backed up by data from several surveys and information agencies, Bonin and Muyskens delivered a devastating critique, scoring textbooks for their gross inaccuracy. The obvious conclusion to be drawn from their work, not only for French but for all foreign langauge teaching, was that teaching materials should provide a statistically accurate picture of the target culture as it really was, and not as authors or students might like to have it. (It is interesting to note, however, that only a few years later the same argument was used by retrenching publishers against feminists demanding less stereotyped treatment of women.)

Conference activity during this period continued to focus regularly on issues of sexism and bias. In 1976 and '77 the Coalition of Women in German, a feminist caucus and allied organization of the AATG and MLA, held special sessions at the AATG national conventions. At the 1977 session Ruth Sanders and Audrone Willeke gave a presentation, later published under the title "Walter ist intelligent und Brigitte ist blond,"[4] which accomplished for German textbooks what Betty Schmitz had accomplished for French ones. In addition, however, Sanders and Willeke suggested specific compensatory strategies which teachers could use to counter the four categories of bias originally defined by Schmitz. As a constructive approach to exclusion, for example, they suggested addition or substitution of reading materials which offered positive female role models or raised issues of special concern to women. To counteract subordination of women, they proposed class discussion and role reversal in dialogues. When the textbook conveyed distorted images of women and men, Sanders and Willeke found it useful to personalize generalizations and to develop students' critical awareness with carefully prepared questions; they took the same approach with degrading or hostile generalizations. In grammar presentations, they recommended varying the order in which neuter, feminine or masculine noun forms were taught; and they noted lexical items

93

that could appropriately serve as points of departure for a discussion of generic masculine or non-parallel treatment of women.

At the 1978 meeting of the Central States Conference, Betty Schmitz updated her analysis and found a marked improvement in the portrayal of female characters, as well as inclusion of more women-related materials.[5] At the 1979 SAMLA conference, Francine Frank and Helen Frink delivered a joint paper, "Sexism in Foreign Language Textbooks,"[6] in which they examined French, Spanish and German texts. Although they, too, saw signs of progress, they concluded that full equality was still a long way off. Ironically, attempts to correct sexism could also create new problems. For example, Frank and Frink noted that many new books were beginning to include passages on the status of women; but in some cases the subject was not taken seriously, and even in the best of cases treatment was little more than tokenism.[7] Moreover, as feminists were beginning to realize, isolation of information about women in a single passage or chapter contributed to the impression that women and women's issues were unrelated to the "mainstream" of cultural history or everyday life. Betty Schmitz, in fact, subsequently developed an analytical category for this problem which she called "Fragmentation/Isolation."[8] Frank also noted that even without overt sex stereotyping or degradation, many textbooks reflected an overwhelmingly masculine world, where only the activities and concerns of men were important.

Besides surveying sexism in foreign language textbooks, Frank and Frink distributed a checklist they had developed for identifying sex bias. This checklist, like the "Suggested Guidelines for Detecting Sexism in French Language Textbooks" distributed by Betty Schmitz at her talk in 1975, called for both quantitative and qualitative analysis of textbooks. The textbook reviewer was asked to count the number of male and female figures, the number of masculine and feminine pronouns that occurred in all sections of the book, and to determine the percentage or ratio of men to women. Male and female characters were to be analysed and tabulated according to profession, behavior, setting in which they appeared and adjectives used to describe them. Both grammar sections and vocabulary were to be examined for a preponderance of masculine forms, for habitual precedence of masculine forms, or for the relegating of feminine forms to stereotypical contexts. Derogatory statements about women could be recorded and numbered These evaluative instruments and others like them were shared via feminist networks all over the United States and helped to sustain the momentum for change.

During this same period, publishing houses began to respond to the feminist critique of their products.[9] Scott, Foresman and Company led the field, issuing its own in-house guidelines in 1972 and 1974. They were followed in 1975 by Ginn and Company, Holt, Rinehart and Winston, Houghton Mifflin, Macmillan, McGraw-Hill and Prentice-Hall. Norton adopted the McGraw-Hill guidelines. After this explosion of concern a few more companies climbed aboard, including Harper and Row (1976), Holt's college department (1976), Random House (1976), Southwestern Publishing Co. (1976), and John Wiley and Sons (1977). Since then, Richard D. Irwin has issued undated guidelines, and in 1981, Houghton Mifflin revised its guidelines, changing the name of the document, significantly enough, from <u>Avoiding Stereotypes</u> to <u>Eliminating Stereotypes</u>.

Thus it would appear that by the late '70s the problem had essentially been solved. School boards had learned to count pronouns, teachers had learned compensatory strategies, authors had been chastized and editors were busy planning non-sexist revisions. But was the problem of sexism in foreign language textbooks really gone? Not really; it had merely assumed more subtle forms. At first glance, the new editions of some of the old offenders provided a pleasant surprise. For example, cosmetic improvements had been made when updating a textbook's illustrations. In dialogues, the ratio of female to male characters had improved, and women now played active as well as passive, supporting roles. The frequency of feminine pronouns in practice exercises had improved; the "Walter ist intelligent, Brigitte ist blond" syndrome had abated, and other gratuitous or unflattering observations about women's habits or appearance had largely been purged. Many books, as mentioned above, had also added material on the position of women in the target culture.

At second glance, it became clear that not all the news was good.[10] Many improvements had been made by deleting material that was clearly offensive. However, addition of new material on women proved more problematical. Furthermore, while some texts did add material, others actually cut material by and about women because of rising production costs, falling demand and the continued feeling that while this information might be interesting and valuable, it remained nonetheless peripheral. Moreover, as Francine Frank pointed out, the publishers' guidelines were rather general, suggestive rather than prescriptive, and none of them applied specifically to the foreign languages. Frank also found enormous inconsistency in the application of guidelines, from publisher to publisher, from language to language, from author to author within a publisher's line, from book to book by the same author(s), and even within the same book. For example, when a textbook was revised, the portions which were rewritten might avoid the use of generic masculine; portions which had not been rewritten, however, would continue to offend. Since Frank made her assessment in 1979, there have been additional developments: computer software coming on the market now is so oblivious to the problem of sexism that it is as if the last decade had never happened; and society's conservative drift has given some publishers an excuse to back off from their earlier commitment. In addition, we still need to reach foreign publishing houses, as well as the producers and distributors of all sorts of ancillary materials, from cultural films and slide shows through film strips, game books, posters and other visuals.

Clearly, neither guidelines nor checklists have outlived their usefulness, and with some refinement they should continue to play an important role in textbook review and revision for years to come. They are the basic instruments of the vigilance Yvonne Rochette-Ozzello has called for. At the same time, though, the checklist-and-guideline approach, like the focus on "sexism," has also revealed certain limits to its usefulness. For one thing, at the classroom level, checklists presuppose an imperfect text and place a tremendous burden of responsibility on the individual instructor, who is obliged to rectify the failings of a particular text with a whole series of thoughtful and effective strategies. For another, checklists evaluate the textbook on an important but ultimately superficial level: they can help us to determine ratios of feminine to masculine pronouns, but can they expose historical inaccuracy, or an overwhelmingly masculine perspective, or elitist values? Unfortunately, such problems do not lend themselves so neatly to this kind of analysis. Checklists sensitized us to the presence of stereotypes and called for their elimination; but checklists have failed to confront the power of stereotypes -- the grain of truth that is contained in them. Checklists called for women professionals and female characters with active, assertive personalities; but checklists did not show us how to look at "typical" female behavior and find the positive qualities in it. Checklists urged us to make lists of derogatory statements about women in textbooks and to demand their removal; but the general bias of the checklist approach was that women should become more like men.

Thus the checklist approach looked at the images of women in textbooks and demanded new images; it did not attempt to revalue traditional images. In the teaching of culture, the checklist approach noted absence of women and lobbied for their inclusion, but according to essentially male notions of accomplishment and greatness or relevance. In the teaching of language, checklists showed that presentations of grammar, vocabulary and usage also reflected discriminatory attitudes toward women; but the checklist approach never called into question the kind of language taught at all. The decade of the '70s focused sharply on educated professional women but paid less attention to other important feminist concerns:racism, classism, homophobia and other forms of marginalization or exclusion from the dominant culture. During this period, feminists in the foreign languages as elsewhere in the women's movement pushed to minimize real or apparent differences between women and men that worked to the disadvantage to women. This was important and necessary work; but the work of maximizing the value of the traditionally feminine remained to be done.

The emergence of women's studies as an academic field made it possible to take this next step. Since the late '60s, women's studies has demonstrated extraordinary productivity and intellectual rigor in the service of a perspective that is uniquely inclusive, egalitarian and humane. The pluralism and sensitivity to difference characteristic of women's studies research and teaching are entirely congenial with the goals of foreign language instruction. In 1980, Yvonne Rochette-Ozzello was the first to make this connection explicitly, when she spoke to the Central States Conference on "Women's Studies and Foreign Language Teaching: A New Alliance."[11] In her talk, which was later published, Rochette-Ozzello argued that when we teach a foreign language and culture, we help to reduce students' ethnocentrism, their tendency to view American culture as the measure of all things. Similarly, she contended, by teaching about women in the foreign language classroom, we can compensate for students' androcentrism, their viewing the male as the measure of all things. Her specific suggestions for the classroom were excellent but not particularly original. The real significance of the talk lay in the linking of women's studies to foreign language instruction. Of course, this connection had been made years earlier for literature classes taught at an advanced level; but Rochette-Ozzello insisted that women's studies was relevant in an even more profound way right at the beginning level, the level at which we reach the largest number of students, female and male alike.

That same year, at the annual AATG meeting in Boston, Women in German sponsored a session on alternative instructional materials. With slides, tapes, and recordings, for example, by feminist pacifist musicians from West Germany, the session became a virtual celebration of the innovative ways in which women could be included in foreign language instruction and particularly in the teaching of culture. The shift in emphasis from grievance to appreciation, from woman as victim to woman as a creative and productive force, however, had even wider implications than this session could suggest.[12]

Research by and about women in art, music and literature, in history, economics and political science, in sociology, psychology, anthropology and many other areas has provided enough theoretical approaches and factual material so that we can at least begin a radical "re-visioning" of the languages and cultures we teach. In practical terms, this means we have new ways of interpreting the old problems-- exclusion, subordination, distortion and degradation -- and new ways to combat them. At the same time, we are now equipped to confront more recently recognized problems: fragmentation, historical inaccuracy, and unreality (the portrayal of complex and controversial social issues in an unrealistically bland and unproblematical, superficial way.[13]

We can counter exclusion and underrepresentation with a growing body of knowledge about women, their lives and their works. Women's studies research has begun to tell us what women's existence as half the human population has meant not only for the elite or public culture of a language group, but also for its private culture: the domestic, material, emotional or religious life of the population. For example, we can make a lesson on Germany's abortive revolution of 1848 more balanced and accurate with an account of the German women's movement born that year, and of the close connection German women perceived then between their personal hopes and the nation's hopes for unity and democracy. And we can point to the dislocation and misery of the laboring classes in German society that subsequently created not only liberal and socialist political parties, but also a bourgeois and a socialist women's movement. Whenever cultural material is presented, either in a textbook or in the classroom, it should be presented with sensitivity to the implications of gender. "Women's issues" should not be isolated in special sections of a textbook or syllabus, any more than women can be separated from humanity. Specifically referring to women and men instead of using the generic masculine -- for example, saying "Arbeiter und Arbeiterinnen" instead of "der Arbeitnehmer" -- forces us to consider whether a generalization really is equally valid for both sexes.

Subordination, like exclusion, is a function of masculine perspective. Women's studies, however, argues for the validity of the feminine perspective: it makes women's invisible sphere visible, and it assigns value to that sphere. What does this mean in concrete terms? A recent Italian textbook[14] devotes several chapters to preparation and anticipation -- by female relatives -- before Beppino, the American cousin, arrives. Are the Italian women thus "subordinated" to Beppino? As the textbook is set up, they are; yet the same incidents could be related in an entirely different way. As the textbook structures the story, we see the visit through Beppino's eyes, but it could also be presented from other points of view. Perhaps there is a great aunt who'll have to do all the cooking for the party in his honor. Of course she's glad to see him, but perhaps she's also wondering how she'll ever fit all this preparation into an already heavy workload. And the aunt -- perhaps she's eager to create for Beppino the pleas-

99

ant illusion that he's the center of all activity, anxious to conceal the business worries that are consuming her and Beppino's uncle. Or the elderly deaf domestic (an object of humor in the book) -- perhaps she hears little but understands even less of what Beppino says because his sentence intonation is off and he never bothers to look at her when he speaks. Or Marcella, his Italian cousin -- perhaps she is annoyed to discover that Beppino has no social conscience and no interest in socialism. But she doesn't want to spoil his visit, so she decides not to talk politics. Beppino's arrival can mean many things to many people; multiple perspectives can give insight not only into gender differences but also into those related to age, class, politics and many other factors. Most American textbooks, today, however, follow one or two main characters -- usually young (male) undergraduates -- through the textbook, and the books inevitably reflect this paucity of viewpoint.

What of stereotyping and distortion? Of course, textbooks should show women in non-traditional jobs, without overpopulating the text to the point of implausibility; and the textbooks should show non-traditional blue-collar and white-collar jobs as well as prestigious professional ones. Most especially, though, we need to reexamine traditional images of women. The problem with stereotypes is not exactly that they are inaccurate, but that they contain just enough truth to seem compelling. Yet stereotypes are distortion, because they simplify and make what is merely common into an emcompassing -- and often oppressive -- generalization. While I do not think textbooks should promulgate stereotypes, I do think textbooks should include images of traditional women, which should be analysed for insights into the target culture and for an appreciation of the genuine values they embody. Take, for example, the conscientious Hausfrau that occurs in a widely used German textbook.[15] Yes, Frau Braun goes to specialty shops several times a week for just the right brand or blend or flavor of whatever. Her behavior, however, is neither silly nor quaint; she goes to these specialty shops for specific practical and emotional reasons. Why does she insist on unground coffee or day-old rye bread? Why does she take her housewifely role so seriously? If we take Frau Braun seriously, we can learn something about the German notion of "Beruf," literally of "calling," in its secular and more-than-secular dimensions. Frau Braun's perception of her role and her dedication to it are related to the German work ethic generally, and we understand all of German society, not just housewives, better when we realize that. Similarly, the concierge, a standard character in French textbooks and a traditional butt of jokes, can be treated with compassion and respect instead: a case history, perhaps, can chronicle her poverty, her pain and her triumphs of survival in a hostile world.

Derogatory generalizations about women have largely disappeared from our textbooks, but the attitudes that inspire them, from sexism through outright misogyny, have not disappeared from the cultures we teach. When our students do encounter such attitudes, whether in literature, art, film or elsewhere, we should sensitize our students and be prepared to discuss the symbols and manifestations of misogyny in the target culture.

The pluralistic approach of women's studies also suggests a way to deal with problems of exclusion or subordination in the teaching of grammar, vocabulary, and usage. Until recently, textbooks tended to be extremely conservative: they taught what was "right" even if it sounded stilted or was no longer in common use. Recent emphasis on "communication" has changed that somewhat, but not to the benefit of women. The fact is, languages are not static; they change and evolve constantly to respond to new needs, and particularly in the ways languages refer to women there is currently a pressing need. Feminists in many countries are working to develop non-discriminatory alternatives to such problems as generic masculine or non-traditional job titles. Some of their coinage may be accepted; other recommendations will not be. There is no reason, however, why a textbook cannot at least acquaint students with this "work in progress," instead of painting a monolithic picture of a language dominated by rules rather than by the people who use it.

The pluralism inherent in women's studies has also made us realize just how narrow the sociological perspective of most foreign language textbooks is. The foreign language textbooks published in the United States today are overwhelmingly populated by an educated, urban upper-middle class. Healthy, attractive young professionals-to-be with politically

and psychologically unproblematical characters attend
university, sit in cafes or travel around the land
of the target culture. Children, the elderly and the
handicapped, the socially disadvantaged and the politically uncomfortable -- all are notable by their
absence. So are crises of any sort: these characters
never seem to suffer a grievous personal loss, a
shattering failure or an economic setback. Nor, for
that matter, do they ever achieve moments of ecstatic
joy, intense satisfaction, significant personal insight or utter hilarity. Linguistically, we find a
bias toward a bland, educated, public, "correct"
language without trace of regionalisms, class characteristics, dialect or intimate usage. Students
learn the vocabulary for socially conservative, politically innocuous behavior, never the vocabulary
of outrage or rebellion. Sociologically, emotionally
and linguistically, these textbooks offer a remark-
ably impoverished slice of life. Is it pure coince-
dence that patriarchal culture has favored the dominant class over the oppressed, the rational over
the emotional, theory over practice and the public
sphere over the private? But the effect of all this
on the language learning process has been to make it
about as inoffensive -- and boring -- as it can become.

The utter absence of any but the mildest emo-
tions in the teaching of foreign language today, however, brings us to another insight, perhaps the most
far-reaching of all, that women's studies has afford-
ed us. Feminist consciousness taught us to look at
the images of women and girls in textbooks with new
eyes and to demand more varied, accurate and humane
portrayal. Women's studies research helped us, particularly in the teaching of culture, to see and
pass on a more balanced picture, one that included
the presence and contributions of women as half
the population. Most recently, however, work by feminist sociolinguists in discourse analysis has given
us new insight into the differences -- real and/or
perceived -- between women's and men's speech. In
other words, a previously unquestioned, invisible
"given" has suddenly become visible.[16]

What we have begun to see, when we look at foreign language textbooks, is that they teach an overwhelmingly "male" use of language. That is, we find
heavy emphasis on transmission of information and
problem-solving, with notable neglect of other uses

of language. In the introduction to their remarkable book, Women and Language in Literature and Society, Sally McConnell-Ginet, Ruth Borker and Nelly Furman write:

"There are important differences among the diverse uses to which language is put... perhaps most surprising to many is the suggestion that 'communication' in the narrow sense of transfer of information is probably not the predominant use of language even outside literary contexts. We flirt, scold, exhort, implore, protest -- and talk just to connect ourselves to others, to reduce our isolation." [17]

In other words, they argue that we use language above all to relate to other people. Looked at in this way, the speech act calls for a different kind of analysis, an analysis of such phenomena as hedges, tag questions or vocalized pauses that do little to advance the transfer of information or solution of problems, but which do convey subtle emotional and relational signals.

It is the "male" uses of language -- impersonal and objective, for information-transfer and problem-solving -- that we have tended to view as the standard for language per se, while "female" uses of language -- indirect and subjective, for expressing emotion or relating to others -- have tended to remain invisible or to be regarded as less valuable uses of language. Of course, men also use "female" language and women use "male" language, so describing them in this way is misleading. But the labelling is accurate in so far as "male" language is perceived as characteristic of men, is viewed as "the real thing" and enjoys higher status and credibility. "Female" language, on the other hand, is perceived as characteristic of women and is less likely to be taken seriously. O'Barr and Atkins[18] suggest that these two styles of speech be called not "women's" and "men's" language, as Robin Lakoff did, but rather "powerful"and "powerless". These descriptive terms, however, fail to acknowledge the positive qualities of the "female"style.

In any case, when we "re-view" foreign language as it is taught in current textbooks from McConnell-Ginet, Borker and Furman's point of view, we suddenly register the absence of countless phenomena

of everyday speech: hedges, tag questions and quali-
fiers, "empty"adjectives, diminutives and super-pol-
ite forms. There are no fillers, bits, vocalized
pauses or curses; we miss exclamations, interjections
and all kinds of spontaneous emotional outbursts. The
characters in textbook dialogues talk blandly and
straightforwardly, proceeding from information transfer to some sort of resolution; in real life, however, our conversations are rarely so orderly or
goal-directed. We make false starts, lose the thread,
are interrupted or diverted. Our "normal" conversations are not linear but meandering or circular; why
else would it be so difficult, in a class or a committee meeting, to conduct an "orderly" discussion?

In fact, textbook dialogues reveal almost nothing of the conversational dynamics which sociolinguists have studied and documented: phenomena such
as topic initiation, interruption, or switch of topic; conversation as a model for competitive or col-
laborative activity; and the sustaining of conversation by means of gambits, links, mediations, leading questions and expressions of interest, encour-
agement, enthusiasm or agreement. Not surprisingly,
gender plays a large role in conversational dynamics.
"Female" speech styles, for example, seem to favor
collaboration, while "male" speech styles encourage
competition for dominance.[19] In single-sex conversation groups, the work of sustaining conversation
may be shared by all; in mixed-sex groups, however,
this "supporting role" seems to fall overwhelmingly
to women. While women's speech may be criticized for
being too indirect, tentative or discursive, these
same qualities can be interpreted positively as tact,
a reluctance to pass judgement and sympathy. Seen
in this light, these speech characteristics may serve
an important function not merely in the sustaining
of conversation but in the sustaining of human relationships.[20]

Yet little attention is paid in most foreign
language instruction to the subtleties, the polite
or deferential forms, indirectness and other qualities which characterize many women's speech, particularly in the expression of opinions, desires
or commands; nor do textbooks explore the implications of diminutive forms or subjunctives. Finally,
there is a vast range of language -- the language
for confiding problems or unloading emotional bur-

dens, the language of intimacy, of newstelling and gossip, of irony, storytelling and bawdy humor -- that is barely tapped for the beginning student. As a result, our students learn a "language" that is bloodless, impoverished and impersonal. If they fail to get excited about the experience, we should hardly be surprised.

Of course I do not wish to suggest a return to gender stereotypes when I argue that this "invisible" realm of language and linguistic interaction be made visible to our students. One of the most interesting findings of recent research is that "male" speech and "female" speech do not in fact differ nearly as widely as they are perceived to differ. Men do make use of "female" speech patterns and vice versa. I would suggest rather that in this area as in others, the emotional/relational should be valued along with the rational; and the roles and responsibilities of linguistic interaction should be shared equitably between women and men, with greater awareness on both sides of the dynamics and implications. If a foreign language textbook can accomplish that for its students, then it has taught them something very powerful indeed.

Since we have only begun to think about this kind of transformation of foreign language instruction, it is difficult to say exactly what a textbook of the future might look like. We can make a few recommendations, though. Most obviously, vocabulary, dialogues and reading passages should deal not only with bland, fact-oriented "public" situations; students should also be exposed to the language of intimacy and emotion. Multiple perspectives should be used to teach about the lives and views of a variety of classes or ethnic minorities in the target culture, and at the same time to expose students to linguistic variety. We could get away from linear conversations, which are rigidly structured and make it almost impossible for students to join in spontaneously. Instead, we could provide circular conversational forms, which would provide multiple openings for a wide variety of comments. For example, a linear conversation begins with an exchange of information and usually ends with some sort of resolution: a decision to go somewhere or do something specific. Each line of the dialogue builds on the line that went before and is the precondition for

the line to follow; students can only use the lines
they have memorized in the "correct" order. Every
language teacher knows the chaos that ensues when
students miss their cues in the recitation of this
kind of dialogue. A circular conversation, on the
other hand, begins with a verbalized situation, for
example, "I've lost it!!"[21] This opens the door to
all sorts of questions, responses and exclamations
from any number of students, in almost any order.
We could also structure conversations around the
notion of dynamics rather than specific content. That
is, we could teach students a series of phrases commonly used to interrupt a conversation, or to introduce a new topic, and then assign roles: "main-
tainers," "interruptors," and so on. The ultimate
benefit of all this for the students would presumably be greater sensitivity to language and heightened
awareness of dynamics, not only in the target language but in the student's native language as well.

There is no need for me to repeat what has
been said so well so many times before -- by Adrienne Rich, Mary Daly and many others -- about the
power that control of language is able to confer. It
follows that when we teach language, either the student's native tongue or a new and "foreign" language,
we are also teaching power -- or continued powerlessness. For us to teach language more successfully, however, several things are necessary. First,
we must dispell the notion, common not only among
authors and editors but students and teachers as
well, that problems of sex stereotyping and the like
have been solved in the newer editions of our textbooks. Treatment of women and minorities has changed,
but it is still highly problematic. Second, it is
essential for all of us working in foreign languages
to understand that women's studies is relevent not
only to advanced-level literature classes; women's
studies perspectives can also make a profound contribution at the ground level of our discipline, the
level at which we encounter the majority of our
students. Finally, we can reassert the centrality of
foreign languages in the liberal arts curriculum.
The place of foreign languages in that curriculum
has become increasingly peripheral and insecure over
the last two decades, the current interest in "core
curriculum" and "central disciplines" notwithstand-
ing. By teaching a richer, more inclusive language
and a better balanced, less politicized view of

human experience, it seems to me that we can stay that drift toward the periphery. We can make the study of foreign language do for the student what we have always claimed it could do -- develop articulateness, discipline the mind, widen horizons and heighten sensitivity -- and do it better than ever.

University of Connecticut

Notes

[1] Sartori-Stein, Anneliese, "Kultureller Chauvinismus im Grammatik-Drill," Die Unterrichtspraxis 32 (1975), pp. 10-20.

[2] Schmitz, Betty, "Sexism in French Language Textbooks," The Cultural Revolution in Foreign Language Teaching,ed. Robert C. Lafayette (Skokie, IL: National Textbook Co., 1975), pp. 119-130.

[3] Bonin, Thérèse and Judith A. Muyskens, "French Women in Language Textbooks: Fact or Fiction?", Contemporary French Civilization #1 (1977), pp. 135-151.

[4] Willeke, Audrone B. and Ruth H. Sanders, "'Walter ist intelligent und Brigitte ist blond': Dealing with Sex Bias in Language Texts," Die Unterrichtspraxis #2 (1978), pp. 60-65.

[5] Rochette-Ozzello, Yvonne, Women's Studies and Foreign Language Teaching: A New Alliance. Women's Studies Research Center Reprint Series #7, University of Wisconsin, Madison (1980), p. 41.

[6] Frank, Francine, "Sexism in Foreign Language Textbooks." Talk presented at annual AATSP meeting, 1980. Unpublished.

[7] Ibid.

[8] Schmitz, Betty, "Instrument for Content Analysis of Sex Bias in Foreign Language Textbooks." (1982). Unpublished.

[9] Frank, Francine, "Guidelines for Non-Sexist Usage; A Preliminary List" (Bibliography). Unpub-

lished.

10 _____ , "Sexism in Foreign Language Textbooks." See also: Jeanette Clausen, "Textbooks and
(In-)Equality: A Survey of Literary Readers for
Elementary and Intermediate German." Die Unterrichtspraxis Vol. 15, No. 2 (Fall 1982), pp. 244-253.

11 Rochette-Ozzello, pp. 37-48.

12 When women's studies began to push for integration of material about women and minorities into
the curriculum all across the liberal arts, it provided still more support for reform in foreign languages. In 1981, and again more strongly in 1982,
the workshops sponsored by Women in German at AATG
conferences stressed that curricular integration and
equity in foreign language teaching materials are
mutually reinforcing. At the 1982 workshop, co-chair-
ed by Betty Schmitz and myself, Peggy McIntosh gave
a keynote address describing the impact that women's
studies is having on traditional disciplines and
emphasizing that curricular integration, like equity
in teaching materials, is no passing academic fad.

13 Schmitz, "Instrument for Content Analysis ...",
p.2.

14 Lazzarino, Graziana, Prego! An Invitation to
Italian (NY: Random House, 1980).

15 Möller, Jack and Helmut Liedloff, Deutsch
Heute (Boston: Houghton Mifflin, 1977).

16 Wright, Barbara, "Achieving Gender-Equity in
Foreign Language Teaching Materials." Talk presented
at Mellon Seminar, Wellesley College, in September
1982 and again at workshop in November 1982.

17 McConnell-Ginet, Sally, Ruth Borker and Nelly
Furman, Women and Language in Literature and Society
(NY: Praeger, 1980), p. xiii.

18 O'Barr, William M. and Bowman K. Atkins,
"'Women's' Language or 'Powerless' Language?" In
McConnell-Ginet et al, p. 93-110.

19 Goodwin, Marjorie Harness, "Directive-Response
Speech Sequences in Girls' and Boys' Task Activities,"
McConnell-Ginet et al, p. 157-173.

[20] Gilligan, Carol, In a Different Voice. Psychological Theory and Women's Development (Cambridge: Harvard University Press, 1982).

[21] I am indebted to Professor Carlos Hortas of Hunter College for this suggestion.

Bibliography

Autorinnengruppe Uni Wien. Das ewige Klischee: Zum Rollenbild und Selbstverständnis bei Männern und Frauen. Hermann Böhlau, 1981.

Bonin, Thérèse and Judith A. Muyskens. "French Women in Language Textbooks: Fact or Fiction?" Contemporary French Civilization, #1 (1977), pp. 135-151.

Butturff, Douglas and Edmund L. Epstein, eds. Women's Language and Style. Studies in Contemporary Language #1, 1978. Available from D. Butturff, Department of English, University of Akron, Akron, OH 44325.

Cassirer, Sidonie, ed. Teaching about Women in the Foreign Languages. French, Spanish, German, Russian. Female Studies IX. Old Westbury, NY: The Feminist Press, 1975.

Clausen, Jeanette. "Textbooks and (In-)Equality: A Survey of Literary Readers for Elementary and Intermediate German." Die Unterrichtspraxis Vol. 15, No. 2 (Fall 1982), pp. 244-253.

Fiske, Edward B. "Scholars Face a Challenge by Feminists." The New York Times, Nov. 23, 1981, p. 1.

Fox, Linda. "Integrating Women's Studies with Hispanic Language and Literature." Talk presented at annual AATSP meeting, 1980.

Frank, Francine Wattman. "Bibliography: Guidelines for Non-Sexist Usage: A Preliminary List." Unpublished.

_____. "Sexism in Foreign Language Textbooks." Talk presented at SAMLA, 1979.

Frazier, Nancy and Myra Sadker. Sexism in School and Society. NY: Harper and Row, 1973.

Frederiksen, Elke. "Women in German Literature: A Different Approach to Teaching Literature." Die Unterrichtspraxis (1978), pp. 39-48.

Graham, Alma. "The Making of a Nonsexist Dictionary." Ms. Magazine, Dec. 1973, pp. 12-14.

Grambs, Jean D. "Sex-stereotypes in Instructional Materials, Literature and Language: A Survey of Research." Women Studies Abstracts I (1972), pp. 1-4, 91-94.

Grünwaldt, Hans-Joachim. "Sind Klassiker etwa nicht antiquiert?" Diskussion Deutsch #1 (1970), pp. 16-38.

Hampares, Katherine. "Sexism in Spanish Lexicography?" Hispania (1976), pp. 100-109.

Jenkins, Mercilee M. and Cheris Kramarae. "A Thief in the House: Women and Language." In Men's Studies Modified. Ed. Dale Spender. NY: Pergamon Press, 1981, pp. 11-22.

Key, Mary Ritchie. Male/Female Language. Metuchen, NJ: Scarecrow Press, 1975.

_____. "The Role of Male and Female in Children's Books--Dispelling all Doubt." Wilson Library Bulletin 46 (1971), pp. 167-176.

Kramer, Cheris, Barrie Thorne and Nancy Henley. Review Essay: "Perspectives on Language and Communication." Signs #3 (1978), pp. 638-651.

Kramarae, Cheris and Paula A. Treichler, eds. Women and Language News. Urbana-Champaign: University of Illinois.

Lakoff, Robin. Language and Woman's Place. NY: Harper and Row, 1975.

Language and Style #4 (1980). Special issue: "Women's Personal and Literary Style." NY: Queens College Press.

Larmer, Larry E. and Mary Badami, eds. Proceedings

of the 2nd and 3rd Annual Conferences on Communication, Language and Gender. Madison: University of Wisconsin-Extension, 1982.

Letts, Janet. "A Bibliography of Scholarship on
Women and French Literature with Evaluations of
its Usefulness to Students at Various Levels of
the Curriculum." FIPSE "Balanced Curriculum"
Grant Project, Wheaton College, Norton, MA (1981).

Mayo, Clara and Nancy M. Henley. Gender and Nonverbal
Behavior. NY: Springer-Verlag, 1981.

McConnell-Ginet, Sally, Ruth Borker and Nelly Furman,
eds. Women and Language in Literature and
Society. NY: Praeger, 1980.

National Education Association. Sex Role Stereotyping in the Schools (1974). Available from: NEA
Order Department, The Academic Building, Saw
Mill Road, West Haven, CT 06516. Cloth: $4.50;
paper: $2.50.

Rochette-Ozzello, Yvonne. "Women's Studies and Foreign Language Teaching: A New Alliance."
Women's Studies Research Center Reprint Series
#7, University of Wisconsin, Madison (1980).

Saario, Terry N., C.N. Jacklin, and C.K. Tittle.
"Sex Role Stereotyping in the Public Schools."
Harvard Educational Review 43 (1973), pp. 386-
416.

Sartori-Stein, Anneliese. "Kultureller Chauvinismus
im Grammatik-Drill." Die Unterrichtspraxis 32
(1975), pp. 10-20.

Schmitz, Betty. "Sexism in French Language Textbooks." The Cultural Revolution in Foreign
Language Teaching. Ed. Robert C. Lafayette.
Skokie, IL: National Textbook Co., 1975, pp.
119-130.

Silberstein, Sandra. Bibliography: Women and Language (Michigan Occasional Papers in Women's
Studies #12). Available from Women's Studies
Program, University of Michigan, Ann Arbor, MI
48109. $2.50.

Spender, Dale. Man-Made Language. London: Routledge Kegan Paul, 1980.

Stefflre, Buford. "Run, Mama, Run: Women Workers in Elementary Readers." The Vocational Guidance Quarterly 18 (1969), pp. 99-102.

Stern, Marjorie, ed. Changing Sexist Practices in the Classroom. Available from American Federation of Teachers, AFL-CIO, 1012 14th St., N.W., Washington, DC 20005.

Stern, Rhoda H. "Sexism in Foreign Language Textbooks." Foreign Language Annals #4 (1976), pp. 294-299.

Thorne, Barrie and Nancy Henley, eds. Language and Sex: Difference and Dominance. Rowley, MA: Newbury House, 1975.

Thorne, Barrie, Cheris Kramarae and Nancy Henley. Language, Gender and Society. Rowley, MA: Newbury House, 1983.

Trömel-Plötz, Senta. Frauensprache in unserer Welt der Männer. Konstanz: Universitätsverlag, 1979.

_____. "Linguistik und Frauensprache." Linguistische Berichte #57 (1978), pp. 49-68.

_____ and Luise Pusch, eds. Linguistische Berichte #69 (1980). Special issue: "Sprache, Geschlecht und Macht I."

_____. Linguistische Berichte #71 (1981). Special issue: "Sprache, Geschlecht und Macht II."

U'Ren, Marjorie B. "The Image of Woman in Textbooks." In Woman in Sexist Society. Ed. Vivian Gornick and Barbara K. Moran. NY: Basic Books, 1971.

Vetterling-Braggin, Mary, ed. Sexist Language: A Modern Philosophical Analysis. Totowa, NJ: Littlefield, Adams, 1981.

Willeke, Audrone B. and Ruth H. Sanders. "Walter is intelligent und Brigitte ist blond: Dealing with Sex Bias in Language Texts." Die Unterrichtspraxis #2 1978, pp. 60-65.

Women in German. "Affirmative Action in the Teaching of German: A Workshop on Erasing Stereotypes." AATG, 1977. Available through ERIC (ED 171 111, 1978, 23 pp.).

Women on Words and Images. Dick and Jane as Victims: Sex Stereotyping in Children's Readers. Princeton, NJ, 1972.

Jeanette Clausen

Broken but not Silent: Language as Experience
in Vera Kamenko's Unter uns war Krieg*

"Whatever is unnamed, undepicted in images,
whatever is omitted from biography, censored in collections of letters, whatever
is misnamed as something else, made diff-
icult-to-come-by, whatever is buried in
the memory by the collapse of meaning
under an inadequate or lying language --
this will become not merely unspoken,
but unspeakable."[1]

The word "unspeakable" may imply one or more of
several meanings: (1) that a thing or event is beyond description, inexpressible; (2) that it is inex-
pressibly bad or objectionable; (3) that is is not to
be spoken. As I understand Adrienne Rich's statement
that the unspoken becomes unspeakable, it encompasses
the whole range of meanings -- impossibility (first
meaning), condemnation or censure (second meaning),
and prohibition (third meaning). Thus, to begin to
"speak the unspeakable" is to do what is impossible
because the words to describe it either do not exist
or their use is prohibited (or both?) as well as to
make oneself a target for censure. Most fundamentally,
then, speaking the unspeakable requires claiming or
creating the language with which to do so.

Vera Kamenko's Unter uns war Krieg,[2] the life
story of a Yugoslavian worker in Berlin, is an un-
usual and important book which exemplifies "speaking
the unspeakable" in both content and form. Vera relates events leading up to the day she beat her seven-
year-old son severely; the following day he had to be
hospitalized and subsequently died. She wrote while
in prison, not in her native language but in German.
As published, the book is the result of collaboration
between Vera and the editor, Marianne Herzog. It con-
sists of Vera's autobiographical narrative (pp.8-82)
plus a few pages of diary entries (pp. 85-98), Marianne's foreword (pp.6-7) and a two-part afterword
(pp. 99-111). The title is taken from Vera's description of the day the beating took place.

In approaching this book, we as readers must con-

115

front many issues, often unspoken, that are basic to feminism: the intersection of multiple oppressions -- based on gender, race or ethnicity, and class -- and the specificity of those oppressions; institutional-ized violence and the use or threat of violence as a means of control; the role of language in an ideology that excludes so-called minorities from full person-hood. I have come to see language not only as a tool, a means for describing and ordering the world and our experiences in it, but also as a continually recur-ring event in our lives, something that happens to us or is done to us as well as something we use and can control. The issue of class is especially im-portant here, for as (relatively) privileged women, we have access to and control over language in a way that a woman like Vera Kamenko does not. Thus, an-other question for us becomes: how do we react to Vera's "broken German"? That is, how does it affect our (potential) relationship to the speaker/writer; does it interfere with or otherwise affect our abil-ity to understand and value her experiences and re-late them to our own?[3] Before discussing these is-sues, it is first necessary to summarize Vera's story.

Vera's Story: Doing the Impossible

"Seid Realisten, verlangt das Unmögliche!"[4]

"I don't believe that idealism is the pri-mary force that moves people. Necessity moves people."[5]

The utopian challenge to "demand the impossible" implies that the only realistic hope for radically changing society lies in doing what is generally be-lieved to be impossible. However, I propose that we also think of this imperative statement in terms of the reality of Vera Kamenko's life, which stands for the lives of many other women who will never get a chance to speak. The utopian demand takes on another dimension when we confront lives that we would prob-ably consider "unlivable," when we remember that millions of such "impossible" lives are being lived every day, through necessity.

Vera Kamenko (b. 1947) tells her life story more or less chronologically, beginning with her childhood in a small Yugoslavian village. She was the only child of her adoptive parents, whom she remembers as

116

basically good, kind people, though quite strict: "Ich glaube, wenn meine Eltern nicht so streng gewesen wären, spätere Missverständnisse und Geschehnisse wären fern geblieben. Ich habe damals gedacht, dass ich im Gefängnis sitze." (VK, p.16). As a young teenager, she runs away from home several times, apparently more on the spur of the moment than by plan. On the second such occasion she is raped by a man she meets in the woods:

"Ich habe nicht versucht zu schreien, weil
sowieso kein Mensch da war....Für mich war
es schrecklich. Nach allem, was geschehen
ist, bin ich mit ihm zusammengegangen, weil
ich Angst hatte, allein im Wald zu sein....
Nachdem was alles mit mir geschehen ist,
konnte ich nicht mehr nach Hause gehen.
Aber ich bin trotzdem nach Hause gegangen.
Es war schon dunkel, und ich hatte Angst,
noch eine Nacht draussen zu bleiben."(VK, p. 19).

I don't think Vera's words "ich konnte nicht mehr nach Hause gehen" should be seen as hyperbole or a "manner of speaking" but as a realistic statement, nor should her calling her parents' home a "jail" be dismissed as cliché. Neither going home nor staying away was a real option. When she does go home, her parents and a doctor who examines her blame her for getting raped; she is held responsible even though she had no control over what happened to her. That such an attitude is widespread does not diminish its significance as a factor in limiting freedom of movement solely on the basis of gender.[6] This experience is repeated with variations numerous times in the course of Vera's life. All her attempts to break away from control and out of confinement end either with her return to the situation she wanted to escape, or to involvement in a different but equally confining situation, often with a man.

At age 17 Vera becomes pregnant, and marries the father shortly before the birth of their son Milorad. Her husband abandons her after a few years. In 1969 she leaves Milorad with her mother and comes to West Berlin to work, anticipating a better life: "Wir haben alle gedacht, dass es für uns in Deutschland leicht zu leben sein wird." (VK, p. 42). Like other foreigners who sign up to work in the FRG, Vera was unprepared for the reality, which is succinctly stated in the Ausländergesetz:

"Ausländer geniessen alle Grundrechte, mit
Ausnahme der Grundrechte der Versammlungs-
freiheit (Art. 8 GG), der Vereinsfreiheit
(Art. 9, Abs. 1 GG), der Freizügigkeit (Art.11
GG), der freien Wahl von Beruf, Arbeitsplatz
und Ausbildungsstätte (Art. 12, Abs.1 GG)
sowie des Schutzes vor Auslieferung an
das Ausland (Art. 16, Abs.2, Satz 1 GG)."[7]

Exceptions like that certainly make you wonder
about the "rights" that do exist. Not to mention the
perverseness of the word "geniessen." On arrival in
Berlin, Vera is immediately confronted with non-
choices: there is no job available for her as Montier-
erin (which she had contracted for) and she must
"choose" between working on the line or taking the
next plane back to Yugoslavia. She and the other women
workers must either abide by the strict rules of the
dormitory or get out. She works in various factories
and sends money to her mother. She is often ill, and
after a year she finds herself laid off from her job
because of illness; she must move out of the dormitory and has neither a place to live nor money.[8] She
moves in with Hasan, a Turkish worker who initially
helps her, but quickly reveals his true colors as a
violent, jealous man:
  "Hasan und ich mussten viel arbeiten, und er
  hatte nichts anderes im Kopf als Sex und
  Essen. Das ist bei ihm das Wichtigste
  gewesen. Er hat mich damals viel geschlagen. Die erste Zeit habe ich gedacht,
  dass er recht hat, aber manchmal bekam
  ich Schläge und ich wusste nicht warum."
  (VK, p.53).

Vera speaks of her life with Hasan as "impossible"
also (e.g. "das war nicht zum Aushalten," VK, p. 61),
but doing anything else seems equally impossible.
She is often ill (as is Hasan); she loses at least
one of her jobs for speaking up about the unfair
treatment she and the other Ausländerinnen receive;
at least twice she tries to leave Hasan, but he
finds her and brings her back. Besides beating Vera,
once nearly strangling her, Hasan abuses Vera sexually and is continually suspicious that she will sleep
with other men.
  "Davon kann nicht die Rede sein. Hasan war
  mir in dieser Beziehung mehr als genug....
  Darum war ich in letzter Zeit krank, ich
  habe Unterleibsschmerzen gehabt." (VK, p.63).

118

It seems almost too obvious to say that control by violence is a lesson Vera has learned all too well on her own body.[9] It is a lesson that continues in prison also, as Vera records in her diary: "Gestern haben mich Bullen geschlagen, weil ich wollte nicht von Freistunde dringehen." (VK, "Gefängnistagebuch," p. 94).

Vera herself doesn't articulate a connection between the abuse she has endured from Hasan (and other men) and her violent attack on Milorad, whom she had brought to live with them in summer 1972, thinking to give him a good education in Germany. However, he can't start school because he speaks no German and must stay alone in the one-room apartment several hours a day while Vera and Hasan are at work. He becomes defiant and resentful. Vera, Hasan and Milorad spend Busstag, a religious holiday in November, alone in the unheated apartment (not realizing it was a holiday, they hadn't bought enough food or coal beforehand). Milorad "macht in die Hose," Vera beats him:

> "Ich habe ihn geschlagen, er hat immer
> weiter freche Worte gesprochen, schmerzende
> Worte für mich, wollte zum Vater, wollte
> zur Schwiegermutter, zur Schule,wollte nicht
> mehr bei mir bleiben. Unter uns war Krieg,
> ich wollte ihn mit Schlägen zum Schweigen
> bringen, er mich mit Frechheit verletzen.
> Diesen Moment vergesse ich nicht. Ich war
> müde von allem und verzweifelt und habe
> einen Menschen geschlagen,den ich liebe.
> Ich habe nachher immer weiter geschlagen,
> ich wusste nicht mehr was ich tue. Ich war
> nicht mehr fähig zum Denken und zum Anhalten,
> bis Hasan mich von ihm weggerissen und in
> den Sessel geschmissen hat." (VK, p. 78).

The next day Vera and Hasan are unable to awaken Milorad from his coma. They take him to the hospital, after Vera has promised Hasan not to testify against him.[10] Vera is arrested. She doesn't find out that Milorad has died until she has been in prison at least a week. She serves three and a half years of her sentence, is released and expelled from the FRG in 1976.

Vera ends her story at the point of her arrest: "Ich bin am Ende meiner Geschichte, ich weiss nicht, was da noch zu schreiben ist. Sie haben mich verhört, ... und ich weiss überhaupt nicht, was ich alles ausgesagt habe. Die deutsche Sprache habe ich nicht

beherrscht wie jetzt...." (VK, p. 82). Vera has, I
think, described her "unspeakable" action as honestly
as any woman could. It is up to us to articulate the
connections between doing the impossible, living unlivable lives, and doing the unspeakable. I expect
that any mother who has ever exploded in anger at
her children will feel a strong connection to Vera,
as I do. Adrienne Rich has said:

> "Powerless women have always used mother-
> ing as a channel -- narrow but deep --
> for their own human will to power, their
> need to return upon the world what it
> has visited on them."[11]

When I first read these words several years ago, I
applied them to the situation of women like myself.
Thinking about them in the context of Vera's life
changes my angle of vision, raises other questions:
have women "always" done this? Is there such a thing
as a "human will to power?" Are such questions even
relevant to the wrongs done to Milorad, Vera, and
also Hasan? I don't think so. Surely the question of
a "human" will to power is irrelevant in societies
based on structural inequalities, where "human" still
basically means "white male." What I do think is important is to understand how the parts of the power
structure (here: employers over workers; Germans over
foreigners; men over women; parents over children)
involve us as women, as mothers, in reproducing conditions that control us by violence or the threat of
violence. Cherríe Moraga, an American Latina whose
experiences are in some ways closer to Vera's than
mine, writes:

> "I have come to believe that the only rea-
> son women of a priveleged class will dare
> to look at how it is that they oppress is
> when they've come to know the meaning of
> their own oppression. And understand that
> the oppression of others hurts them per-
> sonally."[12]

It is easy to say that none of us is free until
everyone is free, but it is harder to understand what
that means in terms of our individual, tangible lives.
I think Vera's story can help us come closer to knowing the meaning of our own oppression. By recognizing
what we have in common with her, especially mothering,
we can see concretely how the oppression of others
hurts us, and potentially our children, personally.
Looking at how we are part of Vera's oppression would

have to include how we do research and teach about women from other cultures, socioeconomic groups, and so on. Marianne Herzog's collaboration on Vera's manuscript can help us here, since she as editor had to grapple with the problematics of class, language and cultural difference.

"Die Mitarbeit." Who is Speaking?

Unter uns war Krieg was published through the efforts of Marianne Herzog, who obtained the manuscript by chance in 1977. Even with her determination to have it appear, the economics of book publishing would probably have thwarted her efforts, had she not received a Literaturstipendium which enabled her to finance a trip to Yugoslavia to work with Vera and devote several months of her time to editing the manuscript. Marianne's criterion in editing was "Verständlichkeit;" her basis for establishing the intended meaning was her tape-recorded line-by-line discussion of the manuscript with Vera. As she explains, she wanted to preserve Vera's manner of writing as much as possible while still making it accessible to a German-speaking public:

"Ich hatte Veras gebrochen deutsch geschriebenes Manuskript und mein Interesse, dass es erscheint. Eine Methode hatte ich nicht. Ich wollte ihren Ausdruck nicht verändern. Erlebte, dass ein der, die oder das, wenn ich es einfügte, aus einem Satz von Vera einen deutschen Satz machte... Las immer wieder Veras Text ohne meine eingefügten Worte. Nach einiger Zeit sprach ich selber gebrochen deutsch. Das ging nicht.... Ich musste auch Sätze neu bilden, die unverständlich waren, und die konnte ich nur in meiner Sprache schreiben und nicht gebrochen deutsch.... Ich habe mitgearbeitet. Ich habe dem Geschriebenen was hinzugefügt: Unabhängigkeit. Ich habe dem Geschriebenen was weggenommen: Auseinandersetzung mit der Sprache, Ungereimtheit, Spannung. Notgedrungenerweise." (VK,"Vorwort," p. 6).

Thus, we have Vera's story in relatively unmediated form, but mediated nonetheless. The longest section (ca.75 pages) of the published work is the chronological autobiography, ending with Vera's ar-

121

rest. This section required the most editing; Marianne supplied chapter divisions, corrected grammar (word order, case, etc.), spelling, punctuation, and, as she says, recast sentences that were incomprehensible. A shorter section (ca. 15 pages), which includes diary entries while in prison and Vera's description of her return to Yugoslavia, is "unedited;" that is, only spelling and punctuation were corrected, not grammar or vocabulary choice (as can be seen by comparing the photocopy of a diary page on the book jacket with the printed text).

Marianne's statement "eine Methode hatte ich nicht" recognizes that traditional methods of research and editing are inadequate for a text like Vera's. Her discovery that supplying definite articles makes "a German sentence" out of one of Vera's sentences provides, perhaps unwittingly, a commentary on the levelling effect of the standard language -- if the grammatical errors are corrected, then Vera's identity as an outsider in Germany is partly obscured. The standard language is inappropriate both to Vera's level of "competence" in German and to her relationship to the language and society as a whole. The editor's dilemma is most poignantly expressed in the word "notgedrungenerweise:" Marianne had to assume that readers would not be willing or able to make the effort necessary to fathom Vera's language without her "intervention." Her comments also acknowledge and respect the differences between her and Vera: she can only write in her own (native) German, not in the "broken German" Vera learned from and with other foreign workers as well as from Germans. Vera's German would inevitably reflect syntactic and semantic characteristics of her own native language, Serbian, as well as patterns common to the German spoken by foreign workers of various nationalities with each other.

Without seeing Vera's original typescript, the answer to the question "who is speaking?" must be: Vera through Marianne. I think it is more important to keep in mind that we, the readers, are the reason for this than to wonder how "authentic" the edited text is. Marianne doesn't give examples of the kinds of sentences in the autobiography that she had to rewrite to make them "understandable." The "unedited" sections, which were mostly written after Vera had already worked for some time on the autobiography, and hence reflect a somewhat stronger command of German, will give readers a degree of insight into the "Auseinandersetzung mit Sprache" which Marianne had to take away from the text in order to give it independence.

Auseinandersetzung mit Sprache, "gebrochen deutsch"

In conversation with Marianne (transcribed in the book's afterword), Vera describes her difficulties in writing German:

> "...damals konnte ich nicht so sprechen wie heute, nicht so schreiben wie heute, viele Worten fehlten....Weil sehr schwer war, auf Papier zu bringen, wann ich sitze und denke, denke, denke,...Sehr schwer, weil diese Gedanken, schon was du gedacht hast, manche sind weggegangen und manche sind dageblieben, ja und dann du musst von vorne denken und aufzuschreiben, und dann natürlich ich habe Buchstaben nicht so an deutsch zu schreiben gewusst,... ich musste immer an Worte denken, wie die schreiben sich, ich konnte mich micht an zwei konzentrieren." (VK,"Arbeit mit Vera," pp. 104-105).

Besides trying to order her thoughts, Vera had to struggle with the language at every level, from the conceptual to the purely mechanical (since Serbian is written in the Cyrillic alphabet, even that was different). When Marianne asks her why she didn't write in her native language, she answers "Ich wollte für mich schreiben, nicht dass einer liest." (VK, "Arbeit mit Vera," p. 105). Though she doesn't say so, it seems that another reason for writing in German is that she experienced events leading up to her imprisonment in German; this situation continued, of course, in prison also. Thus, her "Auseinandersetzung mit Sprache" while writing is a reflection and an extension of her daily struggles to communicate and survive in Germany.

The expression "broken German," generally used in the negative sense of "incorrect, ungrammatical," can be applied in another sense also; Vera "breaks" the language out of necessity, to break the silence. Broken or not, her German was good enough to get her fired from a job. She relates that she complained

123

to factory supervisors that the foreign women, paid
much less than the German women employed there, have
to do most of the work while the German women stand
around and talk. A short time later she is told her
work isn't satisfactory, and is let go:
> "Das war für mich interessant, denn bei
> anderen Firmen waren sie mit mir zufrieden,
> weil ich schnell und gut arbeite und bei
> dieser Firma sind sie es nicht. Bestimmt
> brauchen sie Frauen, welche von der Sprache
> keine Ahnung haben und diese Frauen sollen
> sich totarbeiten." (VK, p. 59).

The correctness of Vera's analysis seems indisputable.
In speaking up about the unfair treatment, she was
breaking the unspoken rules of powerlessness and si-
ence. In her writing, also, she sometimes breaks more
than grammatical rules, by breaking through to an
unspoken level of meaning. For example, in prison
she reflects on how difficult it is to be "vernünftig"
(which implies that she was often admonished to be
so). On one occasion she writes "Ich bin nicht vernünftig sondern ich viel denke." This sentence shows
eloquently, I believe, that Vera understands very
well that being "sensible," vernünftig really means
not to use Vernunft: not to think or to reason, but
to acquiesce, to accommodate oneself to "reality."
Christa Wolf has unmasked the same lying concept in
another way, reflecting on her childhood and training to be "ein vernünftiges Kind:" "Vernunft als
Übereinstimmung...Dämpfer...Einsicht haben und Vernunft annehmen. Auch: zu sich kommen (komm zu dir.)"[13]
An ideology that requires the un-privileged to act
"sensibly" also uses belittling labels, like "broken
German," as one of its tools to keep them in their
place.

A last point I want to bring up about Vera's
struggle to learn and use German is the way it alien-
ates her, at least for a while, from her native language. Immediately upon her release from prison and
return to Yugoslavia, she is taken to the authorities
and interrogated:
> "...und da haben mit Fragereien begonnen.
> Wie warum ich war in Knast undsoweiter,
> ich musste alles erzählen, aber mir war
> sehr schwer zu sprechen, weil ich wieder habe
> jugoslawische Sprache mit deutsch gemischt.
> Und wann ich sagte, ich kann nicht richtig
> an serbisch sagen, was die mich fragten,
> die haben gedacht, dass ich nicht sprechen

will....Haben mir nicht geglaubt, dass mir
richtigen Worten nicht ankommen. Wann ich
sprechen wollte, dann sind deutsche Worten
da und jugoslawische Worten wie weg geb-
lasen. Da habe mich ganz fertig gemacht."
(VK,"Rückkehr nach Hause," pp.97-98).
Language is experience, in a very concrete way. For
almost seven years, Vera had experienced nearly everything in German: work in factories; illnesses;
life with Hasan (she spoke only a few words of Turkish; he spoke no Serbian and thus had no language in
common with Milorad); arrest and sentencing; life in
prison. I point this out not only to "explain" why
she isn't able to speak Serbian when she's interrogated, but to substantiate my assertion that language
is a continually recurring event in our lives. In
my opinion, Vera's book is especially valuable to us
because it allows us to see these aspects of her experience in ways that more conventionally edited
books do not.

Letting Others Speak...

Prevailing attitudes toward "broken" or foreign-
sounding German (or the language of a given dominant
culture) are not easily changed, for reasons all too
familiar to those of us engaged in teaching language
and culture. A recent book about a Turkish woman in
Germany, whose story is similar to Vera's in several
respects, approaches the telling quite differently.
The author, Saliha Scheinhardt, is a Turkish woman
who was educated in Germany. She wrote Frauen, die
sterben, ohne dass sie gelebt hätten[14] on the basis
of what was told her by "Suna S., geborene T.," who
was sentenced to six years of prison in Germany for
killing her husband when she felt she could no longer
tolerate his abuse. Saliha Scheinhardt speaks for
the other woman, in the first person, almost as if
she had assumed her identity.

But Saliha does not speak in a voice entirely of
her own choosing or creation. Rather, Saliha's account of Suna's experiences was meticulously examined and corrected by the book's German editor,
Dietrick Klitzke. In an afterword, "Resümee der Prod-
uktionsgeschichte," he explains:
    "Einmal abgesehen davon, dass die Autorin
    zum damaligen Zeitpunkt noch nicht so in-
    tensiv mit der deutschen Sprache vertraut
    gewesen war, was aber sehr leicht hätte

korrigiert werden können, zeigte es
sich, dass es einen gewaltigen Unterschied geben muss, ob ich 'deutsch denke'
und schreibe oder ob ich 'türkische denke'
und 'deutsch schreibe.' Denn viele Text-
passagen, die uns Deutschen Verständnis-
schwierigkeiten bereiteten, waren für türkische Leser überhaupt kein Problem....
Was war zu tun?...wir wollten an der text-
lichen Eigenart sowenig wie möglich änd-
ern und schon gar keine Eingriffe in
die 'künstlerische Freiheit' vornehmen....
Satz für Satz wurde diskutiert im besonderen
in Hinsicht auf die Verständlichkeit für
das deutschsprachige Leserpublikum....An
manchen Stellen treten auch jetzt noch
Brüche auf, wird der Unterschied zwischen
türkischer Denk - und deutscher Schreibweise überdeutlich. Aber diese Brüche sind
u.E. so gering, dass sie kaum zu Buche
schlagen sollten. Vielmehr sind wir der
festen Überzeugung, dass der von uns
gewählte und beschrittene Weg, die kultur-
elle Eigenart einer türkischen Autorin,
die deutsch schreibt, zu bewahren, eine
Bresche für all jene schlagen wird, die in
dieser 'Zweisprachigkeit' leben, aber
wegen einer Verunsicherung ob des gesell-
schaftlichen 'Perfektionismus-Dogmas' zur
Sprachlosigkeit verurteilt sind, sich
endlich öffentlich zu artikulieren."
(SS, pp. 90-91).

This editorial approach and that of Marianne Herzog
are only superficially similar. Both are concerned
that the text be "understandable" to German readers,
and both make changes. Marianne was reluctant to add
even an omitted "der, die oder das" because it made
a German sentence out of one of Vera's, and she makes
clear that her changes have taken away important aspects of Vera's text ("Auseinandersetzung mit Sprache,
Ungereimtheit, Spannung"). Dietrich Klitzke not only
argues in favor of "Eindeutschung" as the best way
of getting the meaning across, but asserts that this
method will create a "breakthrough" for those still
living between two languages -- a claim that seems
doubtful at best. It almost seems that his intent was
to protect the German readers (or the German language?) from the unfamiliar as much as possible. Some
of his assumptions are highly questionable: is it

possible to work through a text sentence-by-sentence
without influencing "die künstlerische Freiheit"?
(Marianne also went through Vera's text line by line,
but does not claim to leave "artistic license" un-
affected). As for the "Brüche" supposedly still re-
maining in the text -- that is, passages where the
differences between "türkischer Denk- und deutscher
Schreibweise" are apparent -- I am unable to detect
them. Here is a sample of the text:

"Ich hatte tagelang vor dem Wiedersehen
[mit den Kindern] gezittert und hatte
gemischte Gefühle, Angst und Freude zugleich. Ich hatte einige Besorgungen gemacht, Puppen, Süssigkeiten, Autos usw. Im
ersten Moment, als ich sie sah, zitterten
meine Knie, mein Herz schlug, ich wusste
nicht, wie ich sie anreden wollte. Sie
waren so gewachsen und beide sehr hübsch.
Beide redeten mich mit 'Tante' an, ich
war erschüttert. Dann überwand ich mein
Entsetzen. Was sollten sie denn sonst sagen?
Sicher hatten die Kinder erfahren, was geschehen war.
Mein Bruder hatte sicher rücksichtslos und offen den
Kindern das Geschehnis erzählt. Auch die Kinder waren
verblüfft. Sie spielten mit den Geschenken und futter-
ten den ganzeb Tag Kuchen, Obst und Schokolade.
Hin und wieder nahm ich sie in die Arme
und drückte sie ganz fest an meine Brust.
Ich versteckte meine Tränen. Ich habe nicht
gewagt, ihnen zu erzählen, dass ich ihre
Mutter bin." (SS, p. 47).

Suna's first meeting with her children after having been in prison for quite some time is marked by
silence on the subject of her relationship to them:
she doesn't dare tell them she is their mother; she
knows all too well what her sons will have been
taught to think of her. The events and her feelings
are described in simple, short sentences; here, and
often, the book speaks eloquently of Suna's alienation from her accustomed roles, from her culture,
from her very identity (in prison: "...man lernte,
dass man Tag für Tag eine andere wurde." SS, p. 25).
But this alienation is not apparent -- to me -- at
the linguistic level. The language of this text does
not reflect "un-German" usages, structures or idioms,
as Vera Kamenko's much more uneven prose does. Marianne Herzog says of Vera's language: "Die Uneinheit-
lichkeit der Sprache ist Ausdruck der Bedingungen,
ist Ausdruck der Geschichte, unter denen dieses Buch

enstanden ist." (VK, "Vorwort," p. 7). The conditions
under which Frauen, die sterben... was produced
have been largely erased. The book makes a significant
contribution to our understanding of Turkish women's
lives, and to criticize the editorial decision with
respect to language in no way diminishes that contribution. When I think about what I gained from
Vera's and Marianne's collaboration, however, I feel
that the erasure of Suna's and Saliha's struggle with
the language is a loss. The process of their claiming
the language for speaking the unspoken/unspeakable is
invisible. The question as to who is speaking must be
answered even more ambiguously than in Vera's case,
and we as readers do not have (the opportunity) to
confront our own feelings about "thinking Turkish
and writing German" which are part of our (potential)
relationship to women like Suna.

I began my discussion with the proposition that
speaking the unspeakable first and foremost means
claiming or creating the language with which to do
so. In discussing Vera Kamenko's story I have tried
to show how the intersection of oppressions based
on gender, class, and cultural/linguistic difference
makes it both impossible and necessary for Vera to
speak: necessary for us as well as her, so that we
may recognize our own involvement in the structures
that control us as women (with and without privileges
of class or race); impossible without access to "correct" language and the institutions that determine
what will and will not be known. As feminists in academe, we can appreciate and learn from Marianne Herzog's dilemma as editor. Marianne's collaboration
with Vera both enables her to be heard and erases
part of her story -- the "Auseinandersetzung mit
Sprache" which exemplifies Vera's life in Germany as
well as her efforts to write about it. Because this
grappling with language is only partly erased, however, and because Marianne also allows us to see some
of the process she went through in editing the book,
we can see the necessity for questioning our own
biases about "correct" language and our training in
conventional methods of research, editing and also
teaching. Our relationship to "correct" language is
part of our experience, and part of our relationship to Vera and women like her; this aspect of the
relationship is obscured when the language has been
largely standardized, as in the story of Suna S. Our
academic training in what Mary Daly so aptly terms

"methodolatry"[15] has not taught us to let others speak, or even how to listen when they do. In reading the stories of women from whom we are separated by class, race, language, culture (or all of these), we can be guided by these words of Domitila Barrios de Chungara, from the book Let Me Speak!

> "...what I think is that the book is a personal account and should be read from beginning to end without seizing on a single paragraph and interpreting it according to one's own opinion or way of seeing things, but that the book is all related, and it has to be read by understanding it from the beginning to the end. I also think that this account can be a textbook for analysis and criticism, but it's not a question of looking in it for a theoretical position in and of itself. It's an account of my experiences."[16]

I expect that Vera and Suna would concur with Domitila here. If we are serious about uncovering what has been unnamed, distorted, censored or omitted from our knowledge about women, if we are sincere in wanting to let the unspoken become speakable, then I think we ought to take Domitila's advice. By this I do not mean to imply that we should pretend a naiveté we do not feel, or that we should refrain from analysis, interpretation and criticism. But we can gain much by learning to question the assumptions and methods we use in doing these things, so that we do not inadvertently perpetuate the barriers to breaking the silence.

Indiana U.- Purdue U.
at Fort Wayne

Notes

*This paper is the revised and expanded version of a presentation made in the session "Speaking the Unspeakable" at the Seventh Annual Women in German Conference, October 14-17, 1982. I thank Angelika Bammer, whose comments on an early draft of the paper were helpful to me, and the conference participants, whose questions and comments also added much to my thinking.

[1] Adrienne Rich, "It is the Lesbian in Us. . ." (1976), in: Adrienne Rich, On Lies, Secrets and Silence. Selected Prose 1966-1978 (New York: Norton, 1979), p. 199.

[2] Vera Kamenko, Unter uns war Krieg. Autobiografie einer jugoslawischen Arbeiterin. Mitgearbeitet: Marianne Herzog (Berlin: Rotbuch, 1978). Quotations from this book are given in the text of the paper as VK, with pagination.

[3] As I write, I look up words in the dictionary to make sure I am using them in the generally accepted sense, as established by (mostly male) lexicographers. This simple action, one we as academics perform virtually without thinking, seems to me a striking example of the powerful hold "correct" language has over us.

[4] Slogan quoted in: Christa Thomassen, Der lange Weg zu uns selbst. Christa Wolfs Roman "Nachdenken über Christa T." als Erfahrungs- und Handlungsmuster (Kronberg/Ts.: Scriptor, 1977), p. 5.

[5] Charlotte Bunch, "Not for Lesbians Only," in: Building Feminist Theory. Essays from Quest (New York: Longman, 1981), p. 71.

[6] For a discussion of rape as a factor limiting women's freedom of movement, see Susan Rae Peterson, "Coercion and Rape. The State as a Male Protection Racket," and Pamela Soa, "What's Wrong with Rape?" both in: Feminism and Philosophy, ed. Mary Vetterling-Braggin et al. (Totowa, NJ: Littlefield, Adams and Co., 1977). Another valuable discussion of rape is Diane E. H. Russell, The Politics of Rape: The Victim's Perspective (New York: Stein and Day Publishers, 1975).

[7] Verwaltungsvorschrift zu Paragraph 6 (Ausländergesetz), quoted from Courage 4 (April 1978), p. 24. One of the rights the foreign workers do "enjoy" is paying taxes. Cornelia Mansfield points out: "Ausländer zahlen die gleichen Steuern und Sozialabgaben, profitieren aber weniger von ihren Leistungen. Ohne die Beiträge der Ausländer wäre die deutsche Rentenversicherung schon vor 10 Jahren pleite gewesen." Quoted from Courage 4 (April 1978), p. 18.

[8] To realize how desperate Vera's situation was, it is important to remember that she had only a limited work permit at the time, and she did not want to risk being sent back, or deported. The following summarizes some of the obstacles facing foreign women in her situation:

"Arbeitserlaubnis bekommt, wer fünf Jahre rechtmässig und nicht länger als drei Monate unterbrochen gearbeitet hat. Krankheit kann eine Unterbrechung sein. . . . Ist eine Ausländerin länger als ein Jahr arbeitlos, bekommt sie vom Arbeitsamt keine Unterstützung mehr und ihre Aufenthaltserlaubnis wird nicht verlängert--ihr bleibt nur die Rückkehr ins Heimatland. Sie kann auch ausgewiesen werden: Ladendiebstähle oder Verkehrsdelikte sind Grund genug. Eine Ausländerin, die Sozialhilfe erhält, wird ebenfalls ausgewiesen. Ledige und geschiedene Mütter, misshandelte Frauen, sind hiervon am häufigsten betroffen." Quoted from "Initiativen für ausländische Frauen (und Männer)," in: Keiner schiebt uns weg. Zwischenbilanz der Frauenbewegung in der Bundesrepublik, ed. Lottemi Doorman (Weinheim, Basel: Beltz, 1979), p. 347. (emphasis added).

[9] I owe this formulation to Jeannine Blackwell.

[10] Concerning why she makes this promise: the following passage indicates that Hasan, who had beaten Milorad on other occasions, also struck him later the same day:

"Um sieben Uhr haben wir alle beim Fernsehen gesessen und geguckt, . . . [ich] habe nichts gesehen, meine Gedanken waren noch immer bei dem Fall. . . . auf einmal hörte ich, dass beide, Hasan und Mile, zusammen sprachen, und ich hörte einen Knall. . . . [Hasan] hat seine Hand oben gehabt . . . und hat nach unten zum Boden geguckt. Ich habe mich umgedreht und habe Mile am Boden vor dem elektrischen Herd liegen gesehen." (VK, p. 79)

Vera's understandable fear of Hasan, and her horror and guilt feelings about her own actions, doubtless prevented her from being more explicit about Hasan's implication in Milorad's death. Hasan, however, did testify against Vera in court, as we learn from Marianne's afterword (VK, p. 109).

[11] Adrienne Rich, Of Woman Born. Motherhood as Experience and Institution (New York: Norton, 1976; Bantam edition 1977), p. 20.

[12] Cherríe Moraga, "La Güera," in: This Bridge Called My Back. Writings by Radical Women of Color, ed. Cherríe Moraga and Gloria Anzaldúa (Watertown, Mass.: Persephone Press, 1981), p. 33. (italics in original).

[13] Christa Wolf, Kindheitsmuster (Darmstadt: Luchterhand, 1976), pp. 110-111.

[14] Saliha Scheinhardt, Frauen, die sterben, ohne dass sie gelebt hätten (Berlin: Express, 1983). Quotations from this book are given in the text of the paper as SS, with pagination.

[15] Mary Daly, Beyond God the Father: Toward a Philosophy of Women's Liberation (Boston: Beacon, 1973).

[16] Let Me Speak! Testimony of Domitila, a Woman of the Bolivian Mines, by Domitila Barrios de Chungara, with Moema Viezzer. Trans. by Victoria Ortiz (New York and London: Monthly Review Press, 1978), p. 233. This book is also useful for comparison with Vera Kamenko's. It was not written by Domitila, but was assembled from oral interviews with her and speeches she has given. The quoted passage is from the afterword, in which Domitila and her collaborator, Moema Viezzer, discuss the book.

Sources for Further Reading

Articles

"Ausländerinnen in Deutschland," Courage 4 (April 1978), pp. 14-29. Articles on Turkish, Spanish, and Korean women workers in the FRG, and some analysis of specific problems (e.g. battering, Kindergeld).

"Initiativen fur ausländische Frauen (und Männer),"
In Keiner schiebt uns weg. Zwischenbilanz der
Frauenbewegung in der Bundesrepublik. Ed.
Lottemi Doormann. Weinheim, Basel: Beltz, 1979,
pp. 343-352. Three short articles, covers some
of the same information of the April 1978 issue
of Courage already mentioned.

Renate Feyerbacher, "Gegen den Status des 'Gastar-
beiters.' Gleichbehandlung für unsere ausländ-
ischen Mitbürgerinnen und Mitbürger," In Frauen-
programm. Gegen Diskriminierung. Reinbek:
Rowohlt Tb, 1979, pp. 260-266.

Margarete Mitscherlich, "Fremdenhass: Eine Männer-
krankheit?" Emma (April 1982), pp. 36-39.
Focuses mainly on antisemitism, with some reference to similarities to attitudes toward foreign workers.

Books

Baumgartner-Karabak, Andrea and Gisela Landesberger.
Die verkauften Bräute. Türkische Frauen zwischen
Kreuzberg und Anatolien. Reinbek: Rowohlt,
1978. Ser. "Frauen Aktuell." Ed. Susanne von
Paczensky. In two parts: I. "Die Situation der
Frau in der ländlichen Türkei"; II. "Die Situation der türkischen Frauen in Berlin." Part I
based in part on the authors' observations and
experiences during a stay of several months in
Turkey; part II contains statistical information and analysis.

Huth, Christine and Jürgen Micksch, eds. Ausländische
Frauen. Interviews, Analysen und Anregungen für
die Praxis. Frankfurt/M.: Verlag Otto Lembeck,
1982. Interviews and reports concerning Greek,
Turkish and Korean women in the Federal Republic;
examples of projects and services geared especially to the needs of non-German women. A
publication of the Evangelical Church Synod in
Germany (EKD).

Straube, Hanne and Karin König. Zuhause bin ich
"die aus Deutschland." Ausländerinnen erzählen.
Ravensburg: Otto Maier Verlag, 1982. Ser.
"Mädchen und Frauen - Erlebtes, Erzähltes," Ed.
Elisabeth Raabe. Ten interviews with women 13-
22 years old, all of them "second generation,"

i.e. daughters of foreign workers from Greece, Italy, Morocco, Spain, Turkey, Yugosalvia. Authors Straube and König met the women through their work in a social services center for foreigners in Frankfurt.

I am greatly indebted to Judy McAlister-Herman for providing me with many of the sources I consulted for this paper.

Richard L. Johnson

The New West German Peace Movement:
Male Dominance or Feminist Nonviolence

The NATO decision of 12 December 1979 to station 572 medium range nuclear missiles in Western Europe by 1983-84 would be, if implemented, a major step toward the destruction of Europe. This "Nach"rüstungs-beschluss, an alleged catching up with the Russians in response to their stationing of SS-20 missiles, is in fact much more than that. The missiles to be stationed, the American Pershing II and cruise missiles, far outstrip any Soviet weapons in technical sophistication. Pershing II missiles, for example, can travel 1,800 kilometers with an impact accuracy of 30 meters. Although it is true, I believe, that all nuclear missiles are essentially instruments of aggression, not "defense," these new American missiles are among the most obvious examples of attack weapons, whose primary purpose would be to destroy "enemy" missiles before they are launched. The crucial alteration in the balance of terror they provide is clear: for the first time, NATO would have a first strike capacity against the USSR from Europe, primarily the Federal Republic of Germany.

Our major hope for survival is strong national peace movements in NATO and Warsaw Pact countries and international cooperation between them. The new West German peace movement has grown enormously since the NATO "Nach"rüstungsbeschluss. The Krefelder Appell, which calls for a West German decision not to station the Pershing II and cruise missiles, was signed by over 2,500,000 citizens in the FRG by the spring of 1982. The large demonstrations in Bonn, thousands of local peace actions and dozens of acts of civil disobedience at military installations are but the most obvious examples of a growing consensus among West Germans that in a nation which already has the highest concentration of atomic warheads in the world, the stationing of even more would be insane. The Reagan administration scenarios of "flexible response" and "limited nuclear war" in Europe, which have been reported much more extensively in the European press than in the United States, have brought the realization to millions of West Germans

that high level American officials are actively considering a nuclear holocaust which would destroy
Europe forever. All of Europe would be one vast Ausch-
witz.[1]

And yet, precisely at the time when the peace
movement is becoming the most potent extra-parlia-
mentary force in the FRG, the victory in March of
the CDU/CSU and their coalition partner, the FDP,
confirms the power of Helmut Kohl, Reagan's staunch-
est supporter in Europe. Given the presence of a pro-
nuclear coalition in Bonn, it seems to me that the
peace movement must develop two parallel long-term
strategies, whether the Pershing II and cruise missiles are stationed or not: an enormous and growing
autonomous peace movement and the development of a
parliamentary component of that movement.[2] Even
though Kohl is as insulated from the peace movement
as any political leader could be at present, he is
pursuing American and Russian peace talks in large
measure because he realizes that stationing the new
American missiles would probably cause the largest
scale civil disobedience ever in the FRG.[3] Now that
the Greens have cleared the five percent hurdle in
the Bundestag, they will provide a radical presence
for peace that cannot be ignored. I also believe
that the greater the strength of a Basisbewegung for
peace, the greater the chance that the SPD will oppose the stationing of the missiles.[4]

This twin strategy of a mounting extraparliamentary pressure for peace and a coordinated parliamentary initiative requires a unity, and an openness
to diversity, not yet attained in the West German
peace movement. It is the central thesis of this
paper that greater unity is only possible with a
major shift in the peace movement from its present
male dominance toward feminist nonviolence. At present, most male leaders of the peace movement are
caught in a horrendous ideological double-think:
they are publicly opposed to militarism, which at
its core is the most extreme form of patriarchal
dominance, but they themselves reinforce patriarchal
ideology in the movement by excluding women from
positions of power and by a nearly total Totschweigen
of the considerable feminist presence in the peace
movement.

It seems to me that women who are active in
both the autonomous women's movement and the peace

movement provide a model for the peace movement as a whole, a model I feel is best described as feminist nonviolence. I do not believe that any society can have true peace when half of its population is oppressed, and a peace movement must lead the way to liberation by ending male dominance among its leaders and the rank and file. To be sure, there is tension between various movements for liberation; for example, between the peace movement and the ecology movement, as I will discuss later. But in the case of the ecology movement, most peace advocates acknowledge the importance of ecological concerns. The women's movement is the only movement of significance that is totally ignored within the predominantly male leadership of the peace movement.[5]

Feminist theory and practice has proven over the last 15 years that the objective conditions of women's lives can be improved with unified action which recognizes the diversity of women's experience. Although the women's movement did not invent nonviolence, I believe that active nonviolence is an underlying assumption, implicit and explicit, of women's liberation and that this core of nonviolence is particularly evident among the feminists active in the peace movement.[6]

I intend to demonstrate male dominance in Die neue Friedensbewegung, edited by Reiner Steinweg, and to contrast it with a collection by women, Nicht friedlich und nicht still: Streitschriften von Frauen zu Krieg und Gewalt, edited by Ruth-Esther Geiger and Anna Johannesson. Of the wealth of material on the peace movement that has come out in the last three years, these two texts, both published in 1982, exemplify the "zwei Kulturen," as Hanne-Margret Birckenbach calls them, that divide, and could well conquer, the struggle for peace in the FRG.[7] I cannot discuss all of either text, but by focusing on the patriarchal assumptions of Die neue Friedensbewegung and on the goals and means of the women in Nicht friedlich und nicht still, I hope to show how deep the division is between men and women in this movement and then to suggest how the model of feminist nonviolence can make the new West German peace movement the force it must be if nuclear holocaust is to be avoided.

The Steinweg text should be called Die neue

Männerfriedensbewegung. The editorial board of the
Friedensanalysen, the series edited primarily by the
Hessische Stiftung Friedens- und Konfliktforschung
which includes this book, are all men. The board of
the Berghof Stiftung für Konfliktforschung, which
cooperated on the project, are all men. Of the 21
articles in the collection, one is written by a woman, Christiane Rajewsky's "Fünfzig Bücher und sechs
Zugänge zum Thema Frieden: Lesehinweise für Anfänger
und Fortgeschrittene," and one is coauthored by a
woman, Annette Schaub's and Rüdiger Schlaga's
"Verbände, Gruppen und Initiativen der westdeutschen
Friedensbewegung." Each of these articles devotes
one of c. 20 pages to women's contribution to peace.
Schaub's/Schlaga's brief discussion of "Frauen für
den Frieden" is accurate and helpful (pp.392-393).
Rajewsky's entry on Frauen gegen den Krieg, edited
by Gisela Brinkler-Gabler, is the only one she discusses on women and peace. She calls it "eine Fund-
grube antimilitaristischer Texte voller Phantasie,
Sachkenntnis und persönlichem Mut," which is true,
but she also feels it is "eine Überraschung" (p.451).
That comment rankles. The excellence of no other
book, her 50 favorites, surprises her. In these two
articles, women play a peripheral role at best; in
the other 19 authored by men, women play no role at
all. In a book of nearly 500 pages, these two pages
represent less than one half of one percent of the
text.

Steinweg divides the volume into four sections:
Perspektiven, Konstellationen, Internationaler Kontext,
and Zur Praxis. The last section alone would make
it worthwhile. It is packed with information on
peace organizations, initiatives, books and period-
icals, but except for the two pages noted above, one
could easily assume that women do not exist, or are
insignificant, in the West German peace movement.
The "Perspektiven" include no perspective on feminism or nonviolence. In the "Internationaler Kontext,"
which contains articles on the GDR, the Netherlands,
the United States, Great Britain and Italy, one
would conclude that there are no women and certainly
feminists of note in these peace movements either.

I believe the section most useful to discuss
is the "Konstellationen," particularly the three
which Steinweg considers to be the central ones, the
Christian peace movement, the ecology movement and
the unions. These essays provide important insights

into the peace movement as a whole and sufficient material to demonstrate the patriarchal bias of the text.

Hans-Jürgen Benedict in his "Auf dem Weg zur Friedenskirche?: Entstehung und Erscheinungsformen der neuen Friedensbewegung in der evangelischen Kirche" and Lutz Lemhöfer in his "Zögender Aufbruch aus dem Kalten Krieg: Die katholische Kirche und die bundesdeutsche 'neue Friedensbewegung'" agree with many other sources that the Christian component is the most important "Basis" of the West German peace movement and that the Lutheran is far greater than the Catholic contribution. The German word "Basis" is fitting for a number of reasons. It was primarily Christian peace groups that led the earliest initiatives against the NATO "Nach"rüstungsbeschluss; the Christian commitment to peace is a strong movement from below, "von der Basis her"; and Christian faith is an essential ideological underpinning of peace and nonviolence in the FRG.[8]

The Inter-Church Peace Council of the Netherlands, the IKV, provided the most important impetus to the new Christian peace movement in West Germany. In 1977, the IKV published a manifesto with the motto: "Free the world from atomic weapons and begin in the Netherlands." Directly influenced by the IKV, the West German Aktion Sühnezeichen chose a peace campaign for 1980, before NATO's decision to station medium-range missiles, which they called "Frieden schaffen ohne Waffen." At the Kirchentag in Hamburg in June, 1981, 80,000 to 100,000 attended a peace demonstration: "Fürchtet euch -- der Atomtod bedroht uns alle." The gigantic demonstration in Bonn of 10 October 1981 was organized by Aktion Sühnezeichen. In the next month, from November 8-22, 3,000 Lutheran churches in the Federal Republic held peace weeks. I know of no other peace initiatives which can both bring out large numbers of people for demonstrations and organize local actions in 3,000 places at one time over a two-week period.

This activity, which suggests only the most obvious external events in the Christian peace movement in the FRG, was begun by groups outside the Church hierarchies. Using Adrienne Rich's concepts of motherhood as institution and mothering as experience and applying them to a Christian context,

we can see that the official institutions have followed or opposed the experience of individual Christians
and independent Christian peace groups, like Aktion
Sühnzeichen and the even more radical Ohne Rüstung
leben. Thirteen thousand members of the latter group
sent their signatures to Bundesverteidigungsminister
Apel before the "Nach"rüstungsbeschluss, with the
pledge: "Ich bin bereit, ohne den Schutz militärischer
Rüstung zu leben. Ich will in unserem Staat dafür
eintreten, dass Frieden ohne Waffen politisch entwickelt wird." (Benedict, p. 232). It seems to me that
these groups are following Christ rather than the institutions. He lived an exemplary life of action for
peace, as an individual and the leader of a group,
calling for total commitment from his followers to
the spiritual awareness that a Christian must be ready to love her/his "enemy" and to suffer physical
violence without striking back. Going beyond conventional submission to worldly and ecclesiastical authority and anchoring one's path to peace in a direct
experience of Christ are major components in the ex-
ponential growth of the West German peace movement
since 1980.

Harald Müller maintains in his "Ökologiebewegung
und Friedensbewegung: Zur Gefährdung des Lebensraums"
that the ecology movement is a major influence on the
new West German peace movement. Bürgerinitiativen to
improve the deteriorating environment were a powerful
force in the alternative movement of the '70s. Many
peace activists of the early '80s learned how to create effective political groups in the ecology movement, which was itself an heir to the extraparliamentary movements of the '60s, particularly the direct
action to change the structure of the universities
and to end the war in Vietnam. And perhaps most
important to the success of the new peace movement,
it learned from the ecology movement to organize lo-
cally in politically autonomous action groups. One
of the major problems of the peace movement from the
'50s until recently was its strongly centralized organizations and non-existent or relatively weak local chapters.

The participation of leaders like Petra Kelly
and Roland Vogt in both the ecology and the peace
movements strengthens the cooperation between the two.
As Müller states, they are interdependent:
    "Die allgemeinste Grundlage der Gemeins-
    amkeit zwischen Friedens- und Umweltbewälti-

gung ist die Lebensbedrohung, die gleich-
ermassen von moderner Waffentwicklung und
industrieller Grosstechnik ausgeht. In der Ziel-
setzung, eine globale Menschheitskatastrophe ab-
zuwenden, besteht die moralische Identität beider
Überlebensbewegungen' (Roland Vogt). Der
drohende Nuklearkrieg, der das Leben
auf der Erde mit einem Schlag auslöschen
kann, und die schleichende Naturzerstörung
durch hemmungslose Industrialisierung erscheinen dabei nur als zwei Seiten des
gleichen Typus gesellschaftlich-politisch-
wirtschaftlichen Wachstums." (p. 185).
Petra Kelly and Jo Leinen go even further in the book
they coedited, Prinzip Leben: Ökopax -- die neue Kraft,
by asserting, as the word Ökopax suggests, that the
two movements are essentially one. Without denying
that tensions and jealousies exist over whose turf is
whose, Kelly, Leinen and the other contributors demonstrate that peace and harmony with nature are in-
separable.

Of the three central "Konstellationen" in Die
neue Friedensbewegung, the weakest component now
seems to be the unions, as can be seen in Reiner
Steinweg's "Die Bedeutung der Gewerkschaften für die
Friedensbewegung":
"Die Arbeiterbewegung hat in der Geschichte der Friedensbewegung unbestreit-
bar eine enorme Rolle gespielt; zugleich sind Friedensbewegung und Ar-
beiter- bzw. Gewerkschaftsbewegung nie
so ineinander aufgegangen, wie es gele-
gentlich von beiden Seiten behauptet
und gewünscht wird. Das ist heute ange-
sichts einer sich weitgehend aus anderen,
neuen Quellen speisenden Friedensbewegung...noch weniger der Fall als
früher," (p.189).
And yet, as he goes on to explain,
"Dem steht die Beobachtung vieler
Teilnehmer an der grossen Bonner Demonstration vom 10. Oktober 1981 ent-
gegen, dass rund 2000 Busse, die nach
Bonn fuhren, von Gewerkschaftlern gechar-
tert und dass mithin ein gutes Drittel
der Kundgebungsteilnehmer, also mehr
als 100,000, aus dem gewerkschaftlichen
Bereich gekommen sind." (p. 189).
The Deutscher Gewerkschaftsbund plays as hesitant a
role as the church hierarchies in the pursuit of

peace. It is again the movement "von der Basis her" that operates in unions. IG Metall has been the most supportive of the peace initiatives, whereas IG Bergbau und Energie not surprisingly favors increasing nuclear installations in the FRG.

The omission of women from these constellations, both within each one and as an autonomous movement, is glaring. This making women invisible is to me the most pernicious of male strategies to negate women's experience. Outright statements that women belong in the home, though of course reactionary and destructive, can at least be exposed more easily. Steinweg emphasizes that "ein gutes Drittel der Kundgebungsteilnehmer" at the demonstration in Bonn were union members but not that many of the union members themselves and over a third of all the participants were most assuredly women.

I do not have figures on the percentage of women and men involved in the new West German peace movement. But I do know that a clear majority of participants at Lutheran and Catholic services I have attended in the FRG are women. To be sure, the church hierarchies are male, but it is the "Basis" of the churches that carry the Christian movement for peace with them, and the "Basis" is predominantly women. And a significant proportion of women are active in the ecology movement and the unions.

Even though women are trained to submit to the patriarchs in all things, including war, and even though many women have internalized militaristic values, a greater percentage of women than men have supported peace in every opinion poll I have ever read on the subject. Given the constellations discussed in the Steinweg collection and women's traditional opposition to war, we have reason to assume that women are an enormously important foundation of the new West German peace movement.

Steinweg's book is incredibly polished, impersonal, intelligent, and above all, authoritative. Unified in tone, language and approach, the collection contains carefully constructed texts written by academics. It provides an apparently complete rendering of a new movement, a balanced assessment with a wealth of sources. But I felt increasingly uneasy as I read article after article. There were no feelings,

no dialogue. Nuclear holocaust, the most deeply un-
settling specter of our lives, is treated as if it
were a topic of intellectual analysis like any other.
I know that the authors have fears for their lives
and those of their loved ones, and I know that they
have differing views on how to achieve peace. The
problem is that the prevailing norm of scholarly discourse requires the exclusion of feeling and differences of opinion within a text. Anything which breaks
the rule of "objectivity" and reveals the presence
of living, feeling human beings is taboo. The book
is an abstraction away from the pain, conflict and
controversy, a collection of monologues which tend to
cut off debate and discussion. While reading the
book, it is easy to believe that there is only one
way to look at the new German peace movement, their
way. And the book does not move me to action. In fact,
it is consciously written "aus der Distanz der The-
orie." (p. 9).

Nicht friedlich und nicht still puts us in the
middle of a movement, or rather at the vortex of two
movements, the women's and the peace movement. Its
authors are activists who combine theory and practice,
who feel strongly and think clearly. The tone is personal and often oral. Three of the texts were first
presented as speeches, Helke Sander's "Über Beziehungen von Liebesverhältnissen und Mittelstreckenraket-
en," Sibylle Plogstedt's first piece, "Die Angst
zeigen -- die Technik durchschauen," and Eva-Maria
Epple's "'Wehr'-Kraftzersetzung -- Ja!" And the
first contribution is a dialogue, Peggy Parnass' and
Luc Jochimsen's "Frieden Schaffen -- aber wie? Ein
Streitgesprach."

As stated in Geiger's and Johannesson's introduction, the intent of the book is to find common
ground for women by accepting "alle Formen von Protest und Widerstand..., weil nur darin unsere Stärke
liegen kann." (p. 8). The principle of dialogue ex-
tends beyond the first "Streitgespräch." Six other
pieces provide strong ideological disagreements:
Helga Braun's "Ist die Abgrenzungsdebatte in der
Frauenbewegung angekommen?" is a direct response to
Sibylle Plogstedt's second piece, "Ist die Gewalt
in der Frauenbewegung angekommen?", as is Lottemi
Doormann's "Emanzipation wider die Friedfertigkeit?"
to Anna Dorothea Brockmann's "Frauen gegen Krieg,
Frauen für den Frieden -- gegen welchen Krieg, für
welchen Frieden eigentlich?" And although Petra

143

Kelly's "Gewaltfreier Widerstand" is not a direct
reply to a "Stellungnahme" of the Frauen gegen imperialistischen Krieg, it does represent a clearly opposing point of view.

I believe the "eine möglichst grosse Gemeinsamkeit" (p. 8). is attained, in the midst of disagreement, on several issues in part because so many common themes and problems are presented in different
texts. To me, the two central concerns discussed
involve goals -- women's liberation or peace -- and
means -- violence or active nonviolence. On the one
hand, whether a woman should put most of her energy
into the autonomous women's movement or into the
peace movement or whether she should use violent or
nonviolent means, are significant and not always rec-
oncilable. On the other hand, the texts are selected
in such a way that the dialogue between the opposing
views brings new insights and greater involvement
to the reader, And I believe that the selection of
the texts and the explicit position of the editors,
that "die Verbindung zwischen Emanzipation und Anti-
militarismus uns immer lebensnotwendiger scheint,"
(p. 8) give some sense of what goals and means they
and most of the contributors feel will advance the
causes of women and peace.

I turn first to the issue of goals before discussing means. In Nicht friedlich und nicht still
the most pointed disagreement is between Anna Brockmann and Lottemi Doormann. Brockmann's piece is particularly important because of the wide circulation
it has received among West German feminists. It
appeared in shorter version in Courage (2/81) and
Emma (9/81). Brockmann is experienced both in the
autonomous women's movement as an activist at a rape
crisis center in Bremen and in "Aktion Gegenwind,"
which in the summer of 1981 brought women together
to look at planned missile bases in the FRG and to
discuss all forms of male violence in their lives.
She asserts that there is no such thing as peace,
given the daily violence committed by men on women's
bodies and minds, and that women's participation
in any male institution is a betrayal of their experience. "Krieg und Frieden, das sind Kategorien
der männlichen Verbündeten . . . . Mein Alltag als
Frau ist ein beständiger Krieg....Die Kriegsmaschinerie und die Friedensapparate sind nur die mystif-
izierten Superstrukturen derselben Gewalt, die un-

seren Körper einschnürt, unser Leben betäubt, unsere
Utopien erstickt." (p. 110).

Brockmann focuses on male-defined "Friedfertigkeit in Frauen": "In dem auch von uns sorgsam verm-
iedenen Gedanken, unsere Hausarbeit und Liebesarbeit
an Männern tatsächlich aufzukündigen -- als dem viel-
leicht einzigen noch wirksamen Akt von Frauenwider-
stand -- liegt aber auch der Schlüssel für unsere
Möglichkeit, dies zu tun." (p. 109). She therefore
calls for total noncooperation with men in all areas
of life and singles out for criticism women's involvement in peace initiatives with men: "Solange wir
Frauen uns nicht aufraffen können, im alltäglichen
Krieg offensiv zu werden, für unseren Frieden, unsere
Kraft, unsere Fähigkeiten hier und jetzt zu kämpfen,
total zu werden in unseren Forderungen, radikal in
unseren täglichen Handlungen,...traue ich diesen gan-
zen Aufrufen gegen den Krieg und für den Frieden
nicht und sie bleiben kraftlos, sie haben kein Leben;
sie sind halbherzig, weil ohne Konsequenzen, sie sind
ohne Radikalität." (p. 112).

Lottemi Doorman, author of Keiner schiebt uns
weg -- Zwischenbilanz der Frauenbewegung in der Bundesrepublik and co-founder of "Frauen in die Bundes-
wahr? Wir sagen Nein!'," is "erschrocken" by Brockmann's article and highly critical of women who work
exclusively in the women's movement. She sees in
Brockmann a denial of the value of women's work for
peace now and of the work their foremothers have
done:
> "Seit über 60 Jahren', lese ich, wären die
> Aktionen von Frauen gegen den Krieg und
> für den Frieden 'unsichtbar' und 'wirk-
> ungslos' geblieben, weil 'bequem' für die
> Herren und genau das, was sie von uns
> wollen. Welch eine infame Lüge! Warum
> hat die Autorin unterschlagen, dass Frauen
> wegen ihrer angeblichen 'Friedfertig-
> keit', nämlich dem unerschrockenen Kampf
> für den Frieden, in die Illegalität gez-
> wungen wurden und ihr Leben riskiert --
> im ersten Weltkrieg, im Faschismus, im
> Zweiten Weltkrieg? Dass sie für ihre
> 'Friedfertigkeit' verfolgt, verbannt,
> ins Gefängnis gesteckt, gefoltert, um-
> gegracht wurden?" (pp. 119-120).[10]

Whereas Brockmann rejects "Friedfertigkeit" as an
expression of women's oppression, Doormann differ-

entiates between two meanings of the word, between
traditional female passivity and a strong commitment
to peace:
"'Friedfertigkeit' ist kein Wert an sich
und keine angeborene Domäne der Frauen.
Es ist ein Unterschied, ob wir aus 'Friedfertigkeit' Gewalt, Unterdrückung und
Kriege passiv erdulden, oder aus Friedfertigkeit gegen Gewaltverhältnisse,
Mittelstreckenraketen und den Atomkrieg
aufstehen." (p. 121).

For Doormann, there is a radical difference between peace and war, particularly atomic war:
"Dieser geplante Krieg, Schwestern, ist
nicht die einfache Fortsetzung eines
weltumfassenden Geschlechterkampfes,
sondern die äusserste Zuspitzung imper-
ialistischer Gewaltherrschaft in der
Welt: brutalstes Kalkül der Multi-
Rüstungskonzerne und der Weltbeherr-
schungs-Träumer, ausgerechnet mit
Hunderten Million von Toten, gleich ob
Frauen, Kinder oder Männer." (pp. 122-123).

Doormann ends her essay with criticism of a direction in the women's movement which goes far beyond Brockmann:
"Es ist nicht unser Friedenskampf,
der dem Kampf um die Frauenbewegung
schadet. Schädlich ist, wenn sich eine
einflussreiche feministische Zeitung
wie Emma zu einem Blatt entwickelt, das
biedermeierlich die Frauen mit ihren
Problemen unterhält, während draussen
die Apokalypse vorbereitet wird.
Und schliesslich: Ich glaube nicht,
dass der Frieden das ureigenste Interesse nur der Frauen ist. Der Frieden
ist das ureigenste und heute funda-
mentalste Interesse der Menschen, ob
nun Frauen, Männer oder Kinder -- mit
Ausnahme jener Minderheiten von Krieg-
estreibern, die an der AusRüstung der
Menschheit und an millionenfachem Elend,
Hunger und Tod profitiert."(p. 127).

It seems to me that Geiger and Johannesson are
creating a productive dialectic between Brockmann's
and Doormann's approaches. By valuing both posi-

146

tions, the editors demonstrate their confidence in each woman's ability to decide what goals are best for her. And the agreement in the two essays, and the whole book, is substantial: Women must act. In fact, Brockmann and Doormann are both active in the autonomous women's movement and in the peace movement. Geiger and Johannesson seem to be saying: Work for women's liberation, work for peace, and do this either exclusively with women or also with men and children, as you see fit.

One major disagreement in the women's movement-- whether women should join the military and bear arms -- is not, however, treated in the same even-handed way by the editors. It seems to me that Alice Schwarzer's position in Emma,[11] that women's liberation will be advanced by their participation in the military, is hardly represented in the text. Only Luc Jochimsen in the first Streitgespräch presents that point of view. In all the other essays that deal with the issue, Schwarzer's position is strongly opposed. In fact, Johannesson is one of the co-founders of "Frauen in die Bundeswehr -- wir sagen NEIN!" The editors are closer to the position of Courage, that serving in the military is incompatible with the true interests of women. Not only are the editors and most of the contributors ideologically in support of Courage's position, but also Courage is the major single source of the text. Five essays appeared first in Courage. Only one appeared in Emma, Brockmann's, and it appeared first in Courage. Two of the five were written by Sibylle Plogstedt, who is an editor and co-founder of Courage.

Helke Sander's description and rejection of Schwarzer's position is the most concise in the text. It is a position, Sander states, "dass die männliche Macht ihren stärksten Ausdruck in der Militärmaschinerie hat...und dass, um an dieser Macht teilzuhaben, Frauen in sie eindringen müssen, um sie von innen zu durchbrechen...Es ist eine Strategie, die so tut, als könne man auf der Ebene von Putzfrauen einen Konzern übernehmen, um dann mit ihm etwas ganz anderes zu produzieren." (p.70). Hanne-Margret Birckenbach provides to me irrefutable evidence against women's increased participation in the military in several essays cited above. My experience with women and men in the American military indicates that women generally suffer greater

147

oppression there than in other institutions without the slightest chance to change it in a meaningful way. As Birckenbach argues, civilian control of the military is the only viable path to a reduction of militarism. In an opinion poll of Emma readers, 66% stated "Ich bin gegen die Bundeswehr," and among those active in the women's movement, it was 81%. In comparison, only 43% of the readership as a whole and 31% of the activists felt that women should be able to join the Bundeswehr (more than one response was possible for each category).[12] It would appear, then, that the vast majority of Emma readers, particularly the activists, are closer to the predominant view in Nicht friedlich und nicht still than they are to Schwarzer's position. I agree with Sander that Schwarzer may well change her mind as she learns more about the implications of her view.

In nearly every essay in Nicht friedlich und nicht still, the issue of means -- violence or non-violence -- is central. A major difference between Geiger's and Johannesson's and Steinweg's texts has to do with nonviolence, which is as conspicuously absent in the "Perspektiven" and "Konstellationen" of the latter as is the women's movement. I believe that the breadth and depth of thought on nonviolence that Geiger and Johannesson were able to bring together is the most significant contribution of the text.[13] It was one of Gandhi's great insights that goals cannot be understood apart from means. In all nonviolent movements, and I would argue that the essential correspondence between the peace and the women's movement is that they are both inherently nonviolent, the path is the goal. As A. J. Muste said: "There is no way to peace, peace is the way."

Given Geiger's and Johannesson's nonviolent framework, the easy path would be for them to exclude texts that justify or advocate violence. But their confidence in women's ability to decide how they will work for liberation and their belief in the necessity of a wide range of views bring them to include a "Stellungnahme" by "Frauen gegen imperialistischen Krieg" and Ulrike Meinhof's important essay, "Die Würde des Menschen," which appeared in konkret in 1962. They were not, however, able to include the complete statement by "Frauen gegen imperialistischen Krieg":
> "Ihre Schlusspassage zu praktischen Perspektiven eines Friedenskampfes fallen

heute unter die Strafverfolgung nach
129a: Aufruf und Unterstützung einer
terroristischen Vereinigung. Da die
Autorinnen ihren Analyseteil nicht
ohne den Perspektivtext veröffentlichen
wollten, haben sie alles zurückgezogen,
und stattdessen eine Stellungnahme
abgegeben." (p. 9).
Although we do not have their complete statement, we
can gain some insight into their position from the
"Stellungnahme," They maintain,
　　　"dass wir keine 'Friedensfrauen' sind,
　　　weil wir nicht sehen, dass es hier oder
　　　sonst auf der Welt Frieden gäbe und
　　　wir keinen Frieden beschwören können,
　　　sondern nur die Ursachen für Kriege
　　　bekämpfen und zerstören. Wir haben
　　　versucht, durch eine Analyse der imper-
　　　ialistischen Kriegsstrategie, die
　　　gegen die Befreiungsbewegungen in der
　　　3. Welt, gegen die Sowjetunion und
　　　gegen uns, den Widerstand in den
　　　Metropolen des Imperialismus, ger-
　　　ichtet ist, zu begründen, warum wir es
　　　für aussichtslos halten, mit friedlichem
　　　Protest und Verweigerungsaktionen
　　　dieser Kriegsmaschinerie des Imper-
　　　ialismus Einhalt zu gebieten. Warum
　　　wir sagen: Krieg dem imperialistischen
　　　Krieg, und dabei nicht nur einen dro-
　　　henden 3. Weltkrieg vor Augen haben,
　　　sondern den Umsturz eines Systems, das
　　　schon jetzt überall auf der Welt offene
　　　und verdeckte Kriege gegen die Menschen
　　　führt, die sich seiner Herrschaft wid-
　　　ersetzen." (p. 177).
They see clearly the violence of the system of oppression in the "Free World," and they are willing to
support any means necessary, including terror, to
achieve their goal of destroying the system.

　　　Meinhof's article, a brilliant unmasking of the
West German state's betrayal of peace and freedom,
provides implicitly a justification for the approach
taken by the Frauen gegen imperialistischen Krieg and,
of course, for her own development later in the '60s.
She shows that the Grundgesetz was originally "total
freiheitlich und total antimilitärisch": "Demokratie
ist die einzige Menschwürde sichernde Form staatlichen
Zusammenlebens....Krieg ist im 20.Jahrhundert nicht

mehr möglich." (p. 31). But in 1956, the two-thirds
majority in the Bundestag for the "Wehrartikel" con-
firmed Adenauer's support of the Western Allies, and
the "Notstandsgesetz" severely reduced, some would
say destroyed, the individual's right to oppose govern-
mental policies. When the SPD abandoned by 1960 its
previous rejection of atomic weapons, the destruction
of the West German democracy was complete, according
to Meinhof. She cites Robert Jungk. "Atomare Aufrüs-
tung und Demokratie sind unvereinbar," and goes on
to say:

> "Der Satz ist umkehrbar: Atomare Auf-
> rüstung und Auflösung der Demokratie
> bedingen einander zwangsläufig, Mass-
> envernichtungsmittel und Terror ge-
> hören zusammen, technisch, organisa-
> torisch und schliesslich faktisch. Vom
> politischen Programm des Grundgesetz:
> 'Frieden und Freiheit' wäre dann nichts
> übriggeblieben." (p.33).

It would seem to follow, then, in a country with the
highest concentration of atomic weapons in the world
and even more sophisticated "Massenvernichtungsmittel"
on the way, in which peace and freedom have been destroyed and terror reigns, that terror is a neccesary
means to avert total destruction.

If there were only two possible responses to
structural violence, passivity and violence, I would
agree with Gandhi that violence for social progress
would be preferable to submitting to the violence of
the oppressors. But nonviolent action provides a third
path. It seems to me that Geiger and Johannesson included Meinhof's article and the Stellungnahme of the
Frauen gegen imperialistischen Krieg in part because
their analysis of structural violence is so close to
the analysis of nonviolent resisters. The essential
difference is the means.

Petra Kelly's essay, "Gewaltfreier Widerstand,"
is pivotal in Nicht friedlich und nicht still. It is
the most extensive statement on nonviolence in a text
with several contributions to its theory and practice,
particularly Plogstedt's second article, "Ist die
Gewalt in der Frauenbewegung angekommen?", and Helke
Sander's "Über Beziehungen von Liebsverhältnissen und
Mittelstreckenraketen." Kelly's article follows the
Stellungnahme of the Frauen gegen imperialistischen
Krieg and serves as a response to their support of
violent means to liberation. And it is the last es-

150

say in the text. Giving Kelly the last word adds
weight to her statement and supports my contention
that nonviolence is an underlying assumption of the
text.

Kelly's definition of active nonviolence is one
of the most compact I have read, based on her considerable experience in American and European social
and political movements:
> "Die gewaltfreie Aktion ist eine kämpf-
> erische Methode gegen bestehende bzw.
> drohende Formen direkter oder struk-
> tureller Gewalt. Sie gibt nicht nur
> Antwort auf die Frage 'Was tun, wenn
> die Russen kommen?', sondern auch auf
> die zunehmend aktueller werdende Frage
> 'Was tun, wenn die Amerikaner bleiben',
> und gegen unseren Willen neue Mass-
> envernichtungswaffen bei uns bereit
> halten. Gewaltfreie Aktion bedingt
> eine bewusste Entscheidung, jede ihrer
> Handlungen ohne verletzende Gewalt
> gegen Personen durchzuführen. Man kann
> Gewalt nicht durch Gewalt, Krieg nicht
> durch Krieg und die Ungerechtigkeit
> nicht durch Ungerechtigkeit abschaffen.
> (p. 179).

Her emphasis on action "ohne verletzende Gewalt gegen
Personen" is central. In a nonviolent campaign, the
use of force is inevitable. But not violence, not
harming another person. The nonviolent principle of
the least force necessary to create a world without
violence avoids the pitfalls of Friedfertigkeit,
which is such a major concern in the women's movement,
and aggression, the traditional domain of men.

Two insights lie at the core of Kelly's more
concrete suggestions for nonviolent action. Careful
organization is required, and nonviolent resisters
must be willing to break unjust laws when all other
means have been exhausted:
> "Die gewaltfreie Aktion umfasst eine
> breite Skala von steigerungsfähigen
> Verhaltensweisen: vom legalen Protest
> und symbolischen Aufklärungsaktionen
> bis hin zu punktuellen oder das gesamte
> Gesellschaftssystem ablehnenden Kamp-
> agnen zivilen Ungehorsams. Will die
> gewaltfreie Aktion konsequent und

wirksam sein, muss neben die spontane
Entscheidung gegen die Gewalt auch
eine intensive Vorbereitung, Strategie,
Organisation, politische Analyse und
die Formulierung von Fernzielen treten.
Die direkte gewaltfreie Aktion, die
auch Regel- und Gesetzesverletzingen
einschliessen kann, verstehen wir als
letztes Mittel, unseren Standpunkt der
Öffentlichkeit zu vermitteln und Änder-
ungen zu bewirken." (p. 180).
It should be clear that Kelly understands with Meinhof how pervasive structural violence is. And given
the fact that NATO continues to plan the stationing
of the Pershing II and cruise missiles, Kelly's importance as a political figure and her support of nonviolent resistance to a legal escalation of the
threat to peace may well mean a major increase of
civil disobedience in the FRG.

The most widely stated objection to nonviolence
is simply that it is not effective. Kelly addresses
this criticism head on:
"Larzac 1971: Pläne der französischen
Regierung, den Truppenübungsplatz 'Camp
du Larzac' zu erweitern, werden bekannt.
103 betroffene Landwirte schliessen sich
zum 'Bund der 103' zusammen und versprechen,
nicht der Armee zu weichen. Larzac 1981:
Mitterand muss erklären, dass 'Camp du
Larzac' nicht mehr ausgedehnt werde.
Zwischen 1971 und 1981 liegen 10 Jahre.
Widerstand gegen ein gigantisches mili-
tärisches Projekt, das auch die Stationie-
rung der französischen Atomraketen
vorsah." (p. 183).
It is precisely this kind of local action that proves
how effective nonviolent resistance is. And one need
only consider the success of satyagraha in India to
realize that nonviolence works on a large scale as
well.

Kelly sees that nonviolent action illuminates
all aspects of our existence and that it requires
a breadth of vision which most of us are only beginning to attain:
"Im Laufe des Kampfes um Larzac, um
Gorleben, um Kalkar, um Wyhl geht es
dann nicht nur um eine bedrohte Exist-

enz -- sondern auch um neue soziale
Beziehungen, um Selbstentscheidung, um
Selbstverwaltung, um die Emanzipation
der betroffenen Frauen und Männer, um
unabhängige Energiekonzepts für uns und
die Dritte Welt -- es geht um Versöhnung
des Menschen mit sich selbst, Versöhnung
des Menschen mit seiner eigenen Gattung,
mit der Natur, mit dem Kosmos." (p. 183).

Sibylle Plogstedt asserts that feminism is fundamentally nonviolent in her "Ist die Gewalt in der
Frauenbewegung angekommen?". She discusses a utopian
novel by Francoise d'Eaubonne, Les Bergères de l'Apoc-
alypse (Paris, 1977), which contains violence by
women in response to male violence committed against
them: "Ihre Utopie kann man als Anleitung zur Gewalt
lesen. Für mich bedeutete sie aber die eindeutige
Abkehr von Gewalt. Die Gewalt, die von Frauen ausgeht,
ist für mich nicht sympathischer als die, die von
Männern ausgeht." (p. 82). Plogstedt looks back at
her own "Steinwerfen" as a member of the Berliner
SDS and realizes that she had not understood fully
the problem of violence in herself, the student movement, and particularly the RAF. She demonstrates then
essential differences between the RAF and the women's
movement, even though there was solidarity in the
movement for the women in the RAF who were persecuted
and murdered by the government.

Helga Braun's opposition to Plogstedt in "Ist die
Abgrenzungsdebatte in der Frauenbewegung angekommen?"
is, I believe, based on a misunderstanding. Braun
asserts correctly that there is very little physical
violence emanating from the women's movement but assumes incorrectly that Plogstedt is primarily concerned with acts of physical violence among feminists.
It seems to me that Plogstedt is taking on the issue
of violence -- in a feminist utopian novel, in her
own experience, in the women's movement's relationship with women in the RAF -- to develop her analysis
of the women's movement and nonviolence.

To Plogstedt and Kelly, it is not possible to
create a just society by resorting to violent means,
no matter how good the ends might be. Plogstedt
states:
"Ich glaube nicht, dass wir eine neue
Gesellschaft auf einem Gewaltverhältnis
aufbauen können. Weder eine sozialistische

noch eine Frauengesellschaft. In dem
Masse, wie wir Gewalt ausüben, verstossen
wir gegen uns selbst, verändern uns."
(p. 87).
Nonviolence is then an essential model in any movement toward a new society, and Plogstedt locates, as
does Gandhi, the need for nonviolent means not in its
effectiveness in altering external power relations
(although both recognize that), but rather in the
nature of the nonviolent resister, in the essential
humanity of the individual.

Understood from this perspective, nonviolence
does not focus primarily on the "enemy" but rather on
the integrity of the nonviolent resister and the movement s/he creates with others, I find this an incredibly liberating approach to social action and human
nature. In every social movement I have encountered,
there is a tendency to focus one's attention on the
"enemy," not one's own need for liberation as a process of change. In fact, for Gandhi, there was no
such thing as a personal enemy. The primary task of
a satyagrahi was to look within, to uncover untruth
and to become nonviolent in thought, word and action.
A satyagraha campaign would ultimately be successful
if it is just, if the satyagrahis lived for truth
and nonviolence and if they accepted the common humanity in their opponents. Plogstedt, who cites
Gandhi, applies the essential nonviolent principle
that the real enemy is not a person but rather a consciousness, not an individual but rather the role
s/he has taken on:
"Und nun sollen Männer als 'übermächtige'
Feinde an die Wand gestellt werden? Sind
wir so schwach , so verblendet worden,
dass wir nicht mehr erkennen, dass es
um die Funktion der Männer in der Familie,
in den Institutionen, im Staat -- geht?
Um die ganze patriarchale Männerbündelei?
Dass wir die beseitigen, nicht aber den
einzelnen Mann." (p. 88).

Directly related to this discussion of nonviolence
is the feminist unmasking of men's violence against
women, which Plogstedt, Brockmann and Sander in
Nicht friedlich und nicht still and Birckenbach in
"Zur Ignoranz gegenüber der Frauenfriedenbewegung"
address, particularly rape. To me, the unique feminist contribution to the theory and practice of nonviolence is its analysis of, and innovative solutions

154

to, these forms of violence, Combined with the feminist analysis of militarism and the considerable presence of feminists in the peace movement, feminist
nonviolence is the most complete model of social
change I know of in the FRG or any country. To me, the
root of men's denial of women's central role in the
West German peace movement and elsewhere is a more
fundamental denial of women's experience, particularly women's experience of violation by men. As a man,
it is an awesome and difficult process to confront my
participation in male dominance over women. Rape,
battery and pornography, as well as more subtle
forms of violation, don't just happen. They come out
of a dominant consciousness, the same consciousness
that is bringing us so close to nuclear destruction.[14]
To recognize women's role in the peace movement requires that men must abandon "das Wissen von der Inferiorität der Frauen, von der natürlichen Überlegen-
heit des Mannes." (Sander, p. 63).

Men must accept and act on the "kopernikanische
Wende" in sexual politics, in Sander's terms:
"Männer sagen Frauen immer, Männer und
Frauen sollen gemeinsam arbeiten. Man
brauche die Unterstützung aller, um
etwas zu verändern. Der Meinung bin ich
auch. Diese Gemeinsamkeit in den Überle-
bensfragen kann aber für mich heute nur
so aussehen, dass Männer einer feministisch-
en Strategie folgen." (p. 70).
After 15 years of the women's movement, it is time
for us men to follow the feminist model and to apply
it to our social action.

The major reason I argue that men of peace must
become pro-feminist activists is my own experience.
In 1970, after 10 years in the American peace movement, I began to become aware of my oppression of
women. I began to recognize that the peace movement
itself was a bastion of male dominance and that peace
and male dominance are incompatible. Of course, this
recognition is a process. I continue to uncover
patriarchal assumptions in myself, including the
thorny task of how to share fairly housework and
child care while writing this paper.

It is this contradiction between men's critique
of militarism and male dominance in the peace movement that must be overcome. The militarists are wrong,
but consistent. They openly espouse hierarchy. Many

155

men of peace openly espouse egalitarian principles and covertly silence women, denying them leadership in the movement and using them for less prestigious purposes, at typewriters and in beds. I know this is true because I have done it, and I know it is violence against women. Less obvious than rape, battery and pornography, but no less real. And I know it can be stopped.

I see some signs in the new West German peace movement that point the way to accepting women's leadership in autonomous women's groups and in groups with men. For the first time the peace week in October, 1983 will take place with a full day planned by women. And I believe that local groups of nonviolent resisters, as reported by women in the alternative magazine graswurzelrevolution, may well provide a model for action in which men and women work together within a framework of feminist analysis.[15] But the vast majority of men in the movement have not yet accepted women as equals let alone as models for change.

It is difficult for peace activists, men or women, to live nonviolent lives, but I see no other way to convince those who accept stationing of the new missiles that a nuclear free Europe is possible. If activists resort to violence in thought, word or action, why should others take them seriously? But if men working for peace in the FRG learn to apply the principles of nonviolence in their relations with women in all aspects of their lives, the extraparliamentary movement will grow far beyond its already powerful beginnings, and the members of the Bundestag will have to take notice.

Nonviolent action begins with dialog.[16] We must overcome the scholarly, distanced, theoretical mode of writing in Die neue Friedensbewegung and practice the dialogue that permeates Nicht friedlich und nicht still. By basing their book on creative disagreement, Geiger and Johannesson recognize the need for diversity in the women's movement and the peace movement. At the same time, a unity is attained by the common themes discussed and by developing a nonviolent framework. The dialogue between the women in their text provides a model for how the enormous differences in the experience of women and men can be bridged, at least within the peace movement. Listening to others, respecting them even if we choose not to join their

156

group, and renouncing violence are essential to our
path of peace. Women may choose to work only with women, men to work only with men, or there may be women
and men working together, all within the framework of
nonviolent struggle. To me, no one has expressed more
clearly the need for unity and diveristy than Holly
Near:[17]

Unity

Doesn't always mean agreement
It doesn't ever mean the same
Sure doesn't mean burning books and brains
and Jews in Jesus'name
You don't need to rob me
Of the pride that I just found
There's enough love and dignity,
to go all the way around

Chorus:
(So I think we better)
Hang on, don't give up the ship (We're sailing)
Hang on, don't let the anchor slip
We are the sailors and we're in mutiny
The safety of this journey depends on
Unity

It means willing to keep changing
Keeping up to the state of mind
Willing to share the cup
that quenches the thirst of human kind
I never cease to be amazed
When I find that the coast is clear
You see, I'm riding the tail of a mighty whale
And my past has brought me brilliantly to here

Chorus

One man fights the KKK
But he hates the queers (Stop)
One women works for ecology
It's equal rights she fears (Stop)
Some folks know that war is hell
But they put down the blind (Stop)
I think there must be a common ground
But it's mighty hard to find
And the ride is getting rocky
And the ship ain't water tight

157

We better open up our hearts and minds
-- and make room for the speed of light

Chorus

Indiana U.- Purdue U.
at Fort Wayne

Notes

[1] Cf. Jonathan Schell, The Fate of the Earth
(New York: Avon, 1982). His description of nuclear
holocaust and his solutions to this very real danger
for all of us have greatly influenced my vision of a
nuclear free world.

[2] Cf. Hanne-Margret Birckenbach, "Zur Ignoranz
gegenüber der Frauenfriedensbewegung," antimilitar-
ismus information (ami), 13, H. 3 (März, 1983), Y31-
Y36. Birckenbach, a sociologist at the Berghofstif-
tung für Konfliktforschung in Berlin, is the most
knowledgeable and convincing researcher I have found
on a number of issues concerning women and the military. Particularly helpful to me are her "Frauen
und Militär: Keine Männersache," "Frauen, die Lücken-
büsser der Nation?" and "Frauen in der Sprache der
Bundeswehr," all of which appeared in Frauen und
Militär, a special issue of graswurzelrevolution, ed.
Jeannette Kassin and Bernadette Ridard, 8, No. 48
(1980), with the name Hanne Birckenbach, and "'Damit
sie endlich zeigen, was sie überhaupt können' --
Frauenrekrutierung als Militarisierung nach innen,"
in Nicht friedlich und nicht still: Streitschriften
von Frauen zu Krieg und Gewalt, ed. Ruth-Esther Geiger
and Anna Johannesson (München: Frauenbuchverlag,
1982), pp. 128-150.

[3] "Chancellor Helmut Kohl's conservative Government is already bracing for a 'hot autumn' of protest
against the deployment of American medium range missiles. Mr. Kohl is almost desperately eager for a
Soviet-American accord in the Geneva arms talks that
might defuse the planned demonstrations." James M.
Markham, "The Allies Hold Their Breath as Fleet
Moves to Honduras," The New York Times, 31 July 1983,
Sec. 4, p. 3, cols. 1-4. Cf. also Jeffrey Boutwell,

"Politics and the Peace Movement in West Germany," International Security, 7, No. 4 (Spring, 1983), pp. 72-92.

4 The SPD is meeting in November, 1983. Some observers feel the party may oppose the "Nach"rüstungsbeschluss, even though it was ratified by Schmidt while the SPD was in power.

5 In the FRG, an understanding of the role of alternative movements is particularly important. Here, too, the male dominance of the researchers biases the findings. In one of the primary texts discussed here, Die neue Friedensbewegung: Analysen aus der Friedensforschung, ed. Reiner Steinweg (Frankfurt: Suhrkamp, 1982), Peter Schlotter's "Zur Zukunft der Friedensbewegung: Rahmenbedingungen alternativer Politik" is flawed by his total disregard of the women's movement. He finds only "Studenten-, Ökologie-, Friedensbewegung" (p. 19) in the '60s and '70s worth mentioning. Compare Roland Schmidt, "Zur alternativen Kultur: Erscheinungsbild und Strukturen," aus politik und zeitgeschichte, B11 (März 1983): "Die Frauenbewegung war neben der Ökologiebewegung zweifellos die politisch wirkungsvollste Strömung der siebziger Jahre. Ihre Kritik der patriarchalischen Herrschaft in Familie und Beruf stellt das gesamte gesellschaftliche System in Frage." (p. 45)

6 The recognition that the relationship between nonviolence and feminism is central is growing. Cf. Reweaving the Web of Life: Feminism and Nonviolence, ed. Pam McAllister (Philadelphia: New Society Publications, 1982); Feminism and Nonviolence Study Group, Piecing It Together: Feminism and Nonviolence (Devon, England: Feminism and Nonviolence Study Group, 1983). But I would submit that it has been important since the rise of the women's movement in the nineteenth century, often for women in practice more than in theory. Cf. Frauen gegen den Krieg, ed. Gisela Brinker-Gabler (Frankfurt: Fischer, 1980) and Herrad Schenk, "Pazifismus in der ersten Frauen bewegung," in Nicht Friedlich und nicht still, pp. 156-169. Schenk concludes her article with the following sentence: "Frauenbefreiung und Pazifismus sind somit eng verwandte Ziele; gewaltfreier Kampf ist die einzige Möglichkeit, politische Veränderungen herbeizuführen, die die endlose Kette von Gewalt und Gegengewalt durchbrechen." (p. 168). Lida Gustave Heymann

and Anita Augspurg, with Helene Stocker the most important German radical feminist pacifists in the first half of the twentieth century, have much to say about the relationship between pacifism and feminism in Erlebtes-Erschautes: Deutsche Frauen kämpfen fur Freiheit, Recht und Frieden (Meisenheim am Glan: Anton Hain, 1972). Another primary text for me on nonviolence, though it is rarely cited as such, is Virginia Woolf's Three Guineas (London: Hogarth, 1938).

[7] Birckenbach, "Zur Ignoranz gegenüber der Frauenfriedensbewegung," p. Y34. The bibliography by Rajewsky cited above is quite helpful. Cf. also the Buchliste, Antimilitarischer Buchversand & Verlag, Hamburger Allee 49, 6000 Frankfurt 90, and ami, 13, H. 3 (März, 1983), pp. Z21-Z24. Some of the most useful sources of central issues of the new German peace movement as a whole for me are: Frieden mit anderen Waffen: Fünf Vorschläge zu einer alternativen Sicherheitpolitik, ed. Komitee für Grundrechte und Demokratie (Hamburg: Rowohlt, 1981); Alternativen Europäischer Friedenspolitik, ed. Arbeitskreis atomwaffenfreies Europa, n.d.); Alfred Mechtersheimer, Rüstung und Frieden: Der Widersinn der Sicherheitspolitik (München: Wirtschaftsverlag Langen-Müller/Herbig, 1982); Rudolf Bahro, Wahnsinn mit Methode: Über die Logik der Blockkonfrontation, die Friedensbewegung, die Sowjetunion und die DKP (Berlin: Olle & Wolter, 1982); Bernt Engelmann, Weissbuch: Frieden (Köln: Kiepenheuer & Witsch, 1982); Andreas Buro, Zwischen sozial-liberalem Zerfall und konservativer Herrschaft; Zur Situation der Friedens- und Protestbewegung in dieser Zeit (Offenbach: Verlag 2000, 1982); Sozialistische Friedenspolitik: Thesen des Sozialistischen Büros, ed. Arbeitsausschuss, Sozialistisches Büro, (Offenbach: Verlag 2000, 1982); E.P. Thompson, Beyond the Cold War: A New Approach to the Arms Race and Nuclear Annihilation, (New York: Pantheon, 1982); Einmischung in die Politik, special issue of psychosozial, 5, H. 15 (Sept., 1982); Ernest Jouhy, "Die Friedensbewegung und das Problem politischer Wertung, Ästhetik und Kommunikation. H. 50 (Dec., 1982), pp. 86-94.

In addition to Nicht friedlich und nicht still, the most useful sources on the women's peace movement are: Frauen und Militär, cited above; Frauen machen Frieden: Lesebuch für Grossmütter, Mütter und Töchter, ed. Elisabeth Burmeister (Gelnhausen und

Berlin: Laetare, 1981). Cf. also the review, "Frauen und Militär," ami 13, H. 2 (Feb., 1983). Graswurzel-revolution, Courage and Emma all have frequent short articles on women and the military especially since the "Nach"rüstungsbeschluss. Keeping the Peace, ed. Lynne Jones, (Plymouth, England: The Women's Press, 1983) has a section on the women's movement for peace in the FRG as well as in Great Britain, the Nether-lands, Japan and the USA.

8 Of the many sources on the Christian peace movement in the FRG, I would recommend especially: Das Kreuz mit dem Frieden -- 1982 Jahre Christen und Politik,ed. Aktionsgemeinschaft Christentum und Fried-en (Berlin: Elefanten Presse, 1982); Wort an die Ge-meinden zur Kernbewaffnung -- Neue Materialien der Nederlandse Hervormde Kerk, (Neukirchen-Vluyn: Neukirchener Verlag, 1982); Handbuch der Friedensar-beit, ed. Aktion Sühnezeichen/Friedensdienste, Ak-tionsgemeinschaft Dienst für den Frieden (Wuppertal, 1982); Frieden- für Katholiken eine Provokation?: Ein Memorandum, ed. Bensberger Kreis (Hamburg: Rowohlt, 1982).

9 Berlin: Olle & Wolter, 1982.

10 Brinker-Gabler's Frauen gegen den Krieg and Schenk's "Pazifismus in der ersten Frauenbewegung," both cited above, support Doormann's contention that women have been visible and effective in their work for peace.

11 Cf. especially Emma 6/78, 10/79 and 4/82.

12 Frauen und Militär, p. 35, cited above.

13 The single most important German source on nonviolence is Theodor Ebert, Gewaltfreier Aufstand: Alternative zum Bürgerkrieg, 3., erg. Aufl., (Wald-kirch: Waldkircher Verlagsgesellschaft, 1981), which contains an excellent bibliography on nonviolent ac-tion in the FRG and other countries.

14 Birckenbach, "Zur Ignoranz gegenüber der Frauenfriedensbewegung," pp. Y32-Y33.

15 The dialogue between women and men in the Komittee für Frieden, Abrüstung und Zusammenarbeit seems very fruitful to me, as reported in several

issues of graswurzelrevolution. There is no doubt that the men have internalized patriarchal values, but they also accept the need to change in accord with their commitment to nonviolence. The women are actively challenging the men in their groups. Cf. also an article by a man which accepts the need for men to learn from women: "Friedensfrauen," Ästhetik und Kommunikation, 13, H. 47 (Apr., 1982), 118-121.

[16] Dialogue with Angelika Mechtel and Sara Lennox, the materials they shared so freely and their strong commitment to peace have helped me immeasurably in writing this paper.

[17] From her album Speed of Light, (Oakland, Ca.: Redwood Records, 1982). Lyrics by Holly Near, music by Holly Near and Adrienne Torf.